# WhasWasa

# The Whispering of the Shaytan

Imam Abu Abdullah Shams Deen
Ibn Qayyim Al-Juziyyah

Copyright

King Fahd National Library Cataloging-in-Publication Data

All rights reserved. No part of this book may be reproduced or transmitted in any form or by any means, electronic or mechanical, including photocopying, recording, or by any information storage and retrieval system, without written permission from the Publisher.

# Table of Contents

| | |
|---|---|
| Introduction | 5 |
| The Stratagems of the Devil used by the Children of Adam | 6 |
| Satan's Devilish Insinuations | 18 |
| Niyyah in Taharah and Salaah | 35 |
| Excessive use of water in wudu' and bathing | 40 |
| Disregarding any waswasah about breaking wudu' | 43 |
| Things that people are harsh in implementing, while the Prophet ﷺ was indulgent towards himself with them | 45 |
| Some acts that show someone to be an innovator in religion | 46 |
| The way to perform Salaah in shoes | 48 |
| Performing Salaah with shoes on | 49 |
| It is the Sunnah of the Prophet ﷺ to perform Salaah wherever he was | 50 |
| The Companions of the Prophet ﷺ used to walk barefooted to the mosque | 52 |
| What is the Sunnah for when Madhiy[1] touches one's clothes? | 53 |
| Using stones for purification[2], and the ruling regarding pus | 54 |
| Carrying Children during Salaah | 57 |
| The Polytheists' Clothes | 58 |
| The use of water left in open containers | 60 |
| Performing Salaah with a little – but not flowing – blood | 61 |
| Breastfeeding women's clothes | 62 |
| Accepting Food from the People of the Book | 65 |

| | |
|---|---:|
| The similarity between Polytheism and forbidding what is lawful | 66 |
| Waswasah in Pronouncing Letters | 69 |
| Reply to the Excuses of People Under the Influence of Waswasah | 72 |
| Making an oath upon something for divorce | 77 |
| The Ruling Regarding the Doubtful Divorce | 79 |
| Doubts regarding purity | 81 |
| What to do when not knowing the place of an impurity on one's clothing | 83 |
| Confusion in defining whether clothes are pure or impure | 83 |
| Having doubt about the purity of containers used for ablution | 85 |
| Confusion of the direction of the Qiblah | 86 |
| The Confusion of forgetting to pray one Salaah but not knowing which particular one | 86 |
| Invalidating the proofs of people under the influence of waswasah | 88 |
| Waswasah of Ibn 'Umar ؓ in ablution | 89 |
| A reply to those who say that waswasah is better than taking things for granted | 92 |

# The Whispering of the Shaytan

## Introduction

**Bismillah Arrahman Arraheem**

All Praise to Allah Who made Himself known to His close slaves, with the quality of His Sublimity and Majesty, and lit their hearts as they witness the Perfection of His Attributes. He has bestowed upon them His Blessings, and so they believed that He ﷻ is the One, the Self-Sufficient, Who has no partners in His Being, Attributes, or Actions; as He ﷻ has described Himself.

I testify that there is no god worthy of worship but Allah ﷻ, Who has no partners, and I testify that Muhammad ﷺ is His Prophet and Messenger, who was sent as a Mercy to all mankind. He ﷺ is the best of Allah's Creation, the Imam of pious people, a burden for the disbelievers, and a proof for all mankind.

## The Stratagems of the Devil used by the Children of Adam

Allah ﷻ has informed us about His enemy, Iblis (the Satan), when He ﷻ asked him why he refused to prostrate to Adam ﷺ. Iblis argued that he was better than Adam, and asked Allah ﷻ to allow him respite, and He ﷻ allowed him so. Then Iblis, the enemy of Allah, said: ❲Because you have sent me astray, surely, I will lie in wait against them (on) Your Straight Path. Then I will come to them from before them and behind them, from their right and from their left, and you will not find most of them thankful ones❳[1]

The majority of the Interpreters of the Qur'an have explained that Satan's answer was in an ordered manner to show his determination to conspire against the believers.

Ibn 'Abbas ؓ said: "The Straight Path is the clear religion of Allah (Islam)." Ibn Masud ؓ said: "It means the Book of Allah (the Qur'an)." Jabir bin Abdullah ؓ said: "It is Islam." And Mujahid said: "It is the truth."

These are all expressions for one meaning, which is the way to Allah ﷻ.

---

[1] Surat Al-A'raf, verses 16-17.

# The Whispering of the Shaytan

Sabrah bin Al-Faakah reported that the Prophet said: "Satan lies in wait for the children of Adam, using all his (devious) ways."[1]

Ibn 'Atiyyah[2] reported that Ibn 'Abbas said regarding ⟨Then I will come to them from before them⟩, that Satan would try to influence the children of Adam "in their worldly affairs". Ali bin Abi Talhah narrated that the above Verse meant "I will make them have doubt in their Hereafter." This was in agreement with the narration of Al-Hasan, which referred to Satan's attempting to make them (the believers) deny Resurrection, Paradise and Hell.

Mujahid said: "⟨Then I will come to them from before them⟩ means, from where they will be able to view (his devilish temptations)."

⟨and behind them⟩; Ibn 'Abbas said: "It means: 'I will make them strongly desire their world of illusion.'" Al-Hasan said: "I will influence them in their worldly affairs, which I would make appear attractive to them." Abu Salih said: "It means: 'I will make them deny the Hereafter, and distance them from it."

---

[1] An authentic Hadith transmitted by Ahmad, An-Nassai and Ibn Hibban. It was authenticated by Shaikh Al-Albani in "Takhreej At-Targheeb"(2/173).
[2] He is 'Atiyyah bin Sa'd bin Junadah Al-'Awfi Abu Al-Hasan Al-Kufi. He reported from Abu Hurairah, Abu Sa'id Al-Khudri, Ibn 'Abbas. He was considered as weak by Ath-Thawri, Hasheem and Ibn 'Uday, but regarded as sound by Attirmidhi. He died in 111 A.H.

# The Whispering of the Shaytan

Ibn 'Abbas ؓ also said that it meant "I shall make them doubt the importance of their Deen, and good deeds."
Al-Hasan ؓ said that it meant: "I shall make them refrain from doing good deeds."

❬and from their left❭ Al-Hasan ؓ said: "It means: 'I will command them to do evil deeds, which I will make so attractive before their eyes."
Ibn 'Abbas ؓ was authentically reported as saying: "Satan did not say (from above them) because he knew that Allah ﷻ is above them."
Ash-Sha'bi said: "Allah ﷻ bestowed His Mercy to them from above."
Qatadah said: "Satan has come to you, O son of Adam, from all directions, except from above. So he could never stand in your way to achieving the Mercy of Allah."
Al-Wahidi said: "Some people say: 'The right stands for good deeds, while the left stands for bad deeds,' since the Arabs say: 'Place me on your right, but do not place me on your left", which means: 'Make me among your closest people, not among your distant ones."

Al-Azhari reported, quoting other scholars, that Satan made an oath with the Dignity of Allah ﷻ, ❬Iblis said: By Your Might, then I will surely mislead them all❭[1], misleading them all, so that they deny all that was reported of the outcome of previous civilizations, and the

---
[1] surat Sād, verse 82.

# The Whispering of the Shaytan

issue of resurrection, and also confuse people in their daily activities.

Other scholars such as, Abu Is'haq and Az-Zamakhshari, (and the word is that of Abu Is'haq) have said: "All these directions were mentioned for greater emphasis, i.e.: 'I will come to them from all directions.' It could mean, and Allah knows Best, 'I will make sure they are misled from all directions."

Az-Zamakhshari said (interpreting the Verse: "I will come to them from all four directions, from which the enemy usually comes." This is an example of his (the devil's) whisperings and the extent of his influence upon them. Allah ﷻ said in another Verse, addressing Satan: ⟨**Stir up any of them you can with your voice, and rally against them your cavalry and your infantry**⟩[1]

Shaqiq said: "Every morning, Satan lies in wait against me in four observatory places: from before me, behind me, my right, and my left, and says: 'Do not be afraid, for Allah is Most Forgiving, All Merciful.' So I recite: ⟨**And verily, I am indeed forgiving to him who repents, believes and does righteous good deeds, and then remains constant in doing them.**⟩[2] When Satan comes from behind me, he wants to make me worry about the people I will leave behind (when I die), so I recite: ⟨**And no moving (living) creature is there on earth but its**

---
[1] Surah Al-Isra', verse 64.
[2] Surah Ta-Ha, verse 82.

# The Whispering of the Shaytan

provision is due from Allah.⟩¹ When Satan comes to me from my right, he comes to stir my desire for women, so I recite: ⟨The Blessed end is for the pious⟩² and when he comes from my left, he comes to stir all my desires, so I recite: ⟨And a barrier will be set between them and that which they desire.⟩³

I say: "Man follows one of four ways, and none else; he either takes a path on his right, left, in front of him or behind him. On each path, he finds satin lying in wait for him. If man follows any of these paths, while observing the Commands of Allah, he finds Satan laying obstacles against him to stop him from being obedient to Allah ﷻ. But if man follows any of those paths to commit sins, Satan will encourage him and provide all the support he needs.

The following Verse supports the comments of our pious scholars, as Allah ﷻ said: ⟨And We have assigned for them (devils) intimate companions, who have made fair-seeming to them, what was before them and what was behind them.⟩⁴

Al-Kalbi said (it means): "We confine to them some companions among the devils."

---

[1] Surah Hud, verse 6.
[2] Surah Al-A'raf, verse 128.
[3] Surah Fatir, verse 54.
[4] Surah Fussilat, verse 25.

# The Whispering of the Shaytan

Muqatil said: "We prepared for them companions among the devils."

Ibn 'Abbas ؓ said: "What is in front of them (are worldly things), and what is behind them (eternal things of the Hereafter)."

The meaning is: "They made this world fair-seeming to them, until they preferred it to the life of the Hereafter, and even called them to deny it altogether."

Al-Kalbi said: "They made fair-seeming to them what was before them of the matters of the Hereafter) - that there is no Paradise, no Hell-Fire and no Resurrection. (and what was behind them of the matters of this world) - their misguidance in this life."

Ibn Zayd said: "They made all their past evil deeds, and the ones to come, fair-seeming to them." (i.e. the devil made what they were doing seem so attractive to them, that they did not repent for it, and never intended to give up the bad deeds they were ready to commit).

When Satan, the enemy of Allah said: **《Then I will come to them from before them and behind them》**; he meant in this world and the Hereafter; and when he said: **《from their right and from their left》**; he meant 'the angel of good deeds, on the right, urges his person to do good deeds only, so that the devil would have to approach him/her from that side to impede him/her; while the angel

# The Whispering of the Shaytan

of bad deeds, on the left, forbids him/her from doing them, so the devil would have to approach from that side to encourage him/her to do so. All this is summed up in the following Verses:

⟨By Your Might, then I will surely mislead them all⟩[1]
and
⟨They invoke nothing but female deities besides Him (Allah), and they invoke nothing but Satan, a persistent rebel. Allah cursed him. And he (Satan) said: "I will take an appointed portion of your slaves. Verily, I will mislead them, and surely, I will arouse in them false desires and certainly, I will order them to slit the ears of cattle, and indeed I will order them to change the nature created by Allah." And whoever takes Satan as a protector (or helper) instead of Allah, has surely suffered a manifest loss. He makes promises to them, and arouses in them false desires, and Satan promises are nothing but deceptions.⟩[2]

Ad-Dahhak said (it means): "An assumed portion is a known proportion of Allah's slaves."

Az-Zajjaj said (it means): "A proportion that I have appointed for myself."

---

[1] Surah Sâd, verse 82.
[2] Surah An-Nissa', verses 117-120.

# The Whispering of the Shaytan

Al-Fira' said (it means): "The people over whom he (Satan) was made to have authority; so it is like the assumed proportion."

I have said: "The reality of the assumption is that it is an estimation, which means that whoever follows Satan and obeys him, becomes among Satan's appointed proportion of people, who would become his share. For, people are divided into two sections: the followers of Satan, and the followers of the Guidance of Allah ﷻ.

⟨then I will surely mislead⟩
away from the truth, and
⟨surely, I will arouse in them false desires and certainly⟩
Ibn 'Abbas said: "Satan intends to impede the path to repentance."

Al-Kalbi said (it means): "Satan will arouse, in them, false desires and certainty, i.e. there is no Paradise, No Hell-Fire or Resurrection."

Az-Zajjaj said (it means): "He combined misguiding them with arousing in them false desires that they have no fortune in the Hereafter."

It was also interpreted as: "I will arouse in them the urge to follow sinful desires and innovation in religion."

# The Whispering of the Shaytan

And it has been interpreted as: "I will arouse in them the desire to cling to the amenity of this world, until they prefer it to the Hereafter."

❴I will order them to slit the ears of cattle❵
cutting the ears of Al-Baheerah – and this is the word of the majority of the interpreters of the Qur'an. The scholars said that this is also reference to piercing a child's ear, which some of them have allowed for the adornment of a female child only, supporting their opinion with the Hadith of Umm Zar', reported by 'Aishah, may Allah be pleased with her, in which she said, talking about her husband, Abu Zar': "He has given me many ornaments and my ears are heavily loaded with them." The Prophet ﷺ told Aishah, may Allah be pleased with her, after she had related the above Hadith: "I am to you as Abu Zar' was to Umm Zar'."[1]

Imam Ahmad had authorized this for a female child but not the male.

❴and indeed I will order them to change the nature created by Allah❵
Ibn 'Abbas ؓ said: "Satan meant the Religion of Allah", and this is the opinion of Ibrahim, Mujahid, Al-Hasan, Ad-Dahhak, Qatadah, As-Sudday, Sa'id bin Al-Musayyib and Sa'id bin Jubayr.

It means that Allah ﷻ created His servants with a sound nature, i.e. Islam. Allah ﷻ said:

---
[1] Transmitted by Al-Bukhari.

# The Whispering of the Shaytan

❨So set your face firmly towards the Religion (Islam), as a pure natural believer, Allah's natural pattern (Fitrah) on which He made mankind. There is no changing to Allah's creation. This is the true Religion, but most people do not know it. Turning (in repentance) towards Him (only), and be afraid and dutiful to Him.❩[1]

The Prophet ﷺ said: "No child is born except with *Al-Fitrah* (Islam), and then his parents make him Jewish, Christian or Zoroastrian. Also when an animal produces a perfectly formed young one, do you see any part of its body cut? Then he ﷺ recited:
❨Allah's natural pattern (*Al-Fitrah*) upon which He made mankind❩"[2]

The Prophet ﷺ linked two issues: the changing of someone's *Fitrah*, by influencing a child to become Jewish or Christian etc; and by changing of the Creation of Allah, through cutting. These are two things that Iblis (Satan) said he was going to do; so he changed the *Fitrah* of Allah by using Polytheism, and changing their naturally created form (set by Allah ﷻ).

❨He makes promises to them, and arouses in them false desires❩

---

[1] Surah Ar-Rum, verses 30-31.
[2] Transmitted by Al-Bukhari and Muslim, on the authority of Abu Hurayrah ؓ.

# The Whispering of the Shaytan

his promises are those that reach one's heart, such as: 'your lifetime could be extended, so that you would achieve all your desires in this life. You could reach high status, above your own people, and your enemies.' In this manner, Satan increases one's hope, making false promises, and arousing false and diverse desires in one. The difference between what he promises and what he arouses, is that he promises falsehood and arouses non-attainable desires. The base and corrupted self always feeds itself with false desires from Satan; it enjoys living by false hopes.

**⟨Satan threatens you with poverty and orders you to commit *fahsha'* (evil deeds); whereas Allah promises you forgiveness from Himself and bounty⟩**[1]
It is said: 'Satan orders you to commit *fahsha'*, (i.e. to be mean and miserly) (as in this particular verse). Muqatil and Al-Kulabi were quoted as saying, "The term *fahsha'* in the Qur'an means illegal sexual intercourse, except in this context where it means miserliness."

The correct opinion is that the term *fahsha'* is in its general meaning; it refers to every type of *fahisha* (evil deed). It refers to an unmentioned deed, so the attribute carries the general broad meaning of the word.

Therefore, we say that Satan orders mankind to commit evil deeds and among them miserliness. Allah ﷻ has mentioned, in the above Verse, both the threat of Satan

---
[1] Surah Al-Baqarah, verse 268.

# The Whispering of the Shaytan

and his orders. He orders them to commit evil acts and threatens them with evil consequences (if they do good deeds).

These are two things Satan requires of man: he warns them not to commit good deeds, so they abstain from doing them; and he orders them to commit evil deeds which he makes fair-seeming to them, and so they indulge in them easily.

Allah ﷻ then mentioned His Promise, should He ﷻ be obeyed, by those who follow His Commands and avoid His Prohibitions; for which His Promise is His Forgiveness and Bounty. His Forgiveness is protection from evil, while His Bounty is the offering of good. Abdullah bin Mas'ud ﷺ reported that The Prophet ﷺ said: "Satan exercises his influence upon the son of Adam, as does the angel. The influence of Satan is that he holds the promise of evil and denial of truth. And the influence of the angel is that he holds the promise of good and the affirmation of truth. Thus he who perceives this (good promise) should praise Allah and he who finds contrary to it, should seek refuge in Allah from Satan, the accursed. He then recited this verse:
❴**Satan threatens you with the prospect of poverty and bids you to be indecent.**❵"[1]
The angel and Satan take turns with a person's heart like the alternation of the night and day.

---

[1] Recorded by At-Tirmidhi.

# The Whispering of the Shaytan

## Satan's Devilish Insinuations

One of the stratagems of Satan is to whisper to Muslims in matters of ritual purification (like ablution) and *Salaah*, when they intend to perform them. He manages to keep them away from following the *Sunnah* of the Prophet ﷺ, by making them believe that all the teachings in the *Sunnah* are not enough to worship Allah ﷻ properly; so they try to invent other methods, hoping to increase the reward from Allah ﷻ, while they, in fact, are reducing it or even cancelling it out altogether.

There is no doubt that it is Satan who calls people to follow wicked thoughts and temptations; it is wicked people who have obeyed Satan, embraced his call, and followed his command. They rejected the *Sunnah* of the Prophet ﷺ, to the extent that someone thought that if he performed ablution in the manner of the Prophet ﷺ and washed like him, he would still not be able to cleanse himself properly.

The Prophet ﷺ used to perform *Wudu'* (ablution) with a quarter of Syrian *ratl*[1], and washed his body with one *ratl* and a quarter. A person who is under the influence of the devil's inspiration would see that measure as not even enough to wash his hands. It was authentically reported that the Prophet ﷺ performed the steps of ablution one by

---

[1] Syrian measure equal to 3.202kg (3.202 litres of water).

# The Whispering of the Shaytan

one, and would not exceed beyond three times for a particular step. He ﷺ even mentioned that: "Whoever exceeds this has transgressed and acted unjustly." The person under the influence of *waswasah* is a transgressor, as testified by the Prophet ﷺ. Therefore, how could we possibly get closer to Allah ﷻ with acts that transgress beyond His boundaries?

It was also reported that the Prophet ﷺ used to perform *Ghusl* (the major ritual ablution of the whole body) with 'Aishah ﵂ using just one large bowl, in which some traces of dough remained. If the person, under the influence of Satan, heard of someone doing likewise, he would object to him, saying: "This is not enough for two people to wash properly!"

The Prophet ﷺ used to wash using one large bowl not only with 'Aishah ﵂ but with his other wives, such as Maimunah and Umm Salamah.

Ibn 'Umar ﵂ was also quoted as saying: "During the Prophet's lifetime, husbands and their wives used to perform ablution using one single bowl."

The guidance of the Prophet ﷺ states that it is permissible to wash from a container, even if it is not full of water; and whoever does not wash unless the basin is full of water and does not let others share it with him, is indeed transgressing the *Sunnah* of the Prophet ﷺ.

# The Whispering of the Shaytan

Shaikh Ibn Taymiyah (may Allah bless him) said: "It needs more strength to scold such people from legislating beyond the Divine Legislation of Allah ﷻ; for they worship Allah ﷻ with their innovations, not by following the *Sunnah* of His Prophet ﷺ.

This authentic Sunnah confirms that the Prophet ﷺ and his Companions ﷺ did not waste water by pouring it abundantly, and this was also the practice of their Followers.

Sa'id bin Al-Musayyib (may Allah bless him) said: "I used to perform ablution from on single container, and would leave some for my wife."

Imam Ahmad (may Allah bless him) said: "A knowledgeable person should only use a small quantity of water."

When the Prophet ﷺ performed ablution or washed all his body, he used to put his hand inside the container to get water; he would rinse his mouth and wash his nose. The person under the influence of Satan's whisperings would not agree; he would most likely consider that water as impure, and would never share one container with his wife! He would feel disgust at the thought of it, the way the disbeliever feels when Allah's Name is mentioned.

People under the influence of Satan's whisperings may say: "We carry out these precautions for the Sake of our Religion; implementing the sayings of the Prophet ﷺ:

# The Whispering of the Shaytan

"Leave what causes you doubt, and turn to what does not cause you doubt,"[1] and "Whoever saves himself from the suspicious things, saves his religion and his honour,"[2] and "A sin is that which weaves in the heart of someone."

Some scholars of the past have said: "A sin leaves the heart in perplexity and anxiety." The Prophet ﷺ passed a date fallen on the way and said: "Were I not afraid that it may be from a *Sadaqah* (charitable gifts), I would have eaten it."[3] Has the Prophet ﷺ not abstained from eating the date as a precaution?

Imam Malik gave a *fatwa* (legal opinion) with regards to a person who divorced his wife and had doubt, whether it was the first or third pronouncement of divorce, that it should be considered as the third pronouncement of divorce, as a precaution to prevent any illegal sexual relations occurring (between the man and his divorced wife).

He also gave a *fatwa* concerning a man who divorced one of his wives yet forgot (that he had divorced her), that all his wives should automatically be divorced from him, as a precaution against his forgetfulness; a preventive measure against doubt.

---

[1] Recorded by Imam Ahmad, on the authority of Anas ﷺ. Also recorded by An-Nassai, At-Tirmidhi who said: it is sound and authentic, and Ibn Hibban, on the authority of Al-Hasan bin Ali ﷺ.
[2] Recorded by Al-Bukhari, Muslim, Abu Dawud and At-Tirmidhi, on the authority of An-Nu'man bin Bashir.
[3] Recorded by Al-Bukhari, on the authority of Anas ﷺ.

# The Whispering of the Shaytan

If a man should say to his wife: "At the end of the year, you will be fully divorced (three times)," then she should be divorced from him there and then (i.e. at the time of his saying so), as this is a preventive measure.

The scholars have also said, in this context of precautionary measures, that whoever misses the spot of impurity in his garment, should wash the whole of it.

The scholars have said that if a person was wearing clean garments and one of the garments should become impure, yet he has doubt as to which one it was, then he may perform *Salaah* wearing a garment over the impure one (depending on the number of impure spots), and perform an extra *Salaah* for certainty; to relieve his conscience.

The scholars said that if clean vessels were mixed and confused with impure ones, one should avoid all of them and perform *tayammum* instead. Also if one is confused about the direction of the *Qiblah*[1], then one should perform four *Salaah*s according to some scholars, to relieve one's conscience with certainty.

They have said: "Whoever did not perform a particular *Salaah* in a day, and forgot about it, should perform all five *Salaah*s of that particular day again."

The Prophet ﷺ has commanded that whoever has doubt in his *Salaah*, should make decisions based on certainty (i.e.

---
[1] Direction in which Muslims turn while praying, towards the Ka'bah.

# The Whispering of the Shaytan

acting according to his certainty). He ﷺ forbade Muslims from eating game if one was not sure whether the prey was hit by him or by someone else, and also if it fell into water.

These are some examples in the long topic of doubtfulness and precaution.

Precaution and acting according to certainty is not rejected in Islam, even if some people like to call it *waswasah*!

If we take precautions for ourselves and act only according to our certainty, by leaving what causes us doubt, and turning to what does not cause us doubt, and by avoiding suspicious things, we would certainly not be outside the teachings of the *Shari'ah*, nor be indulging in the world of *bid'ah* (innovation). This is better than one taking things for granted, acting carelessly, regarding one's religion, such as not paying attention to the amount of water one uses for *wudu'*, or in what place one performs *Salaah*, or one's purity of clothes; such a person does not care about suspicious things, and considers everything as pure, even if doubtful.

They said: "All they object from us are the precautionary measures we take in performing an obligation or avoiding a forbidden one. This is better than acting carelessly with regard to both; because it often leads to shortcomings in one's obligations, and involvement in forbidden things.

# The Whispering of the Shaytan

Allah ﷻ has said:
❨Indeed, in the Messenger of Allah you have a good example to follow for him who hopes for Allah and the Last Day, and remembers Allah much❩¹

❨Say: If your really love Allah, then follow me, Allah will love you❩²

❨and follow him so that you may be guided❩³

❨and verily, this is my Straight Path, so follow it and do not follow other paths❩⁴

The Right Path that Allah ﷻ Commands us to follow is that of the Prophet ﷺ, which was followed by his Companions ﬞ. Yet whatever objective deviates from it is a form of transgression. Nevertheless, transgression can either be serious or less so; and between the two, there are levels of transgression that can only be measured by Allah ﷻ.

Therefore, the scale with which one can use to identify righteousness from transgression is the Sunnah of the Prophet ﷺ and his Companions ﬞ.

---
¹ Surah Al-Ahzab, verse 21.
² Surah Al-'Imran, verse 31.
³ Surah Al-A'raf, verse 158.
⁴ Surah Al-An'am, verse 153.

# The Whispering of the Shaytan

A transgressor may be unjust (an oppressor), a *Mujtahid*[1], or a *Muqallid* (a person who blindly imitates others). Among these are some who either deserve punishment or forgiveness, yet some of them may even be rewarded once according to their intentions and effort in their worship of Allah ﷻ.

The guidance of the Prophet ﷺ, as practised by his Companions ﷺ, shows which of the two ways are best to follow.

One should be reminded of the prohibition of exceeding one's proper limits, and of extravagance in Islam, and that thriftiness and observing the Sunnah are central objectives of the *Deen*.

Allah ﷻ has said:
⟨**O people of the Book, do not exceed the limits of your religion**⟩[2],

⟨**And do not waste by extravagance**⟩[3],

⟨**These are the limits ordained by Allah, so do not transgress them**⟩[4],

---

[1] A legist formulating independent decisions in legal or theological matters, based on the interpretation and application of the four school of fiqh (Islamic Jurisprudence).
[2] Surah An-Nisa', verse 171.
[3] Surah Al-An'am, verse 141.
[4] Surah Al-Baqarah, verse 229.

# The Whispering of the Shaytan

⟨do not transgress the limits. Truly, Allah does not like the transgressors⟩[1],
and
⟨invoke your Lord with humility and in secret. He does not like aggressors⟩[2]

Ibn 'Abbas said: "In the morning of Al-Aqabah, the Prophet said to me, while he was mounting his camel: 'Pick up some stones for me'. So I collected seven stones for him. He then started shaking them in his hand and said: 'Such people (who exceed the boundaries of Allah), you should aim at.' Then he said: 'O people, beware of excessiveness in religion; for people before you were destroyed by their excesses in religion.'"[3]

Anas said: "The Prophet said: 'Do not impose austerities on yourselves so that austerities would be imposed on you. For people who have imposed austerities on themselves, Allah has imposed austerities on them; their survivors are to be found in cells and monasteries. Then he quoted:
⟨Monasticism, they invented it, We did not prescribe it for them.⟩"[4]

The Prophet forbid austerity or severity in religion, by exceeding what is prescribed in Islam. He also

---

[1] Surah Al-Baqarah, verse 190.
[2] Surah Al-A'raf, verse 55.
[3] Recorded by Ahmad and An-Nassai.
[4] Recorded by Abu Dawud, and this Hadith is considered weak.

# The Whispering of the Shaytan

informed that a person's austerity on himself is the cause of Allah's austerity on him, either by *qadar* (Divine Decree) or by *shar'* (Islamic Legislation).

Austerity by *Shar'* is when someone imposes severity on himself, with a heavy pledge, and commits himself to it

Austerity by *qadar* is when someone is under the influence of Satan's whisperings.

Al-Bukhari said: "People of knowledge disliked excess in *wudu'*, and exceeding the practice of the Prophet ﷺ. Ibn 'Umar ؓ said: 'Performing ablution properly is purity.'"

Therefore, *fiqh* – all aspects of *fiqh* – is economy in religion and adherence to the *Sunnah*.

'Ubay bin Ka'b said: "Follow the Path and Sunnah (of the Prophet ﷺ); for any servant of Allah who follows the Path and the Sunnah (of the Prophet ﷺ) remembers Allah ﷻ, and his body shivers out of fear from Allah ﷻ; his sins would be removed, the way leaves are wasted away from their dry tree. Economising in a path or a sunnah of the Prophet ﷺ is better than an individual interpretation in a particular dispute in Sunnah. So, make sure that your economy in your activities is according to the practice of the Prophet ﷺ."

Shaikh Abu Muhammad Al-Maqdisi said in his book *"Dham Al-Muwaswiseen"*:

# The Whispering of the Shaytan

"All Praise to Allah Who guided us with His Blessings, and honoured us with Muhammad ﷺ and his Message. He ﷻ helped us follow the Sunnah of His Prophet ﷺ and made a sign to have the Love and Blessing of Allah ﷻ bestowed upon us. He ﷻ said:

❮Say: "If you really love Allah, then follow me, Allah will love you and forgive you your sins. And Allah is Oft-Forgiving, Most Merciful❯[1],

❮and My Mercy embraces all things. I shall ordain it to those who are the pious, who give Zakat, and believe in Our Signs; those who follow the Messenger, the Prophet who can neither read nor write❯[2],

❮So believe in Allah and His Messenger, the Prophet who can neither read nor write, who believes in Allah and His Words, and follow him so that you may be guided❯[3].

Verily, Allah ﷻ has made Satan an enemy to Man; he lies in wait against him in the Right Path, and comes to him from every direction and path, as we have been informed by Allah ﷻ:

❮Because you have sent me astray, surely I will lie in wait against them on Your Straight Path. Then I will come to them from before them and behind them,

---
[1] Surah Al-'Imran, verse 31.
[2] Surah Al-A'raf, verse 156-157.
[3] Surah Al-A'raf, verse 158.

# The Whispering of the Shaytan

from their right and fro their left, and you will not find most of them thankful ones⟩¹.

Allah ﷻ warned us against following him (the devil) and commanded us to be his enemy and opponent; He ﷻ said:
⟨Surely, Satan is an enemy to you, so take him as an enemy⟩²,

⟨O Children of Adam, do not let Satan deceive you as he got your parents out of Paradise⟩³

Allah ﷻ informed us what Satan did to our Parents (Adam and Eve ﷺ); to warn us against obeying him, and to invalidate any excuse if we should choose to follow him. He ﷻ commanded us to follow His Right Path and forbade us to take different paths; He ﷻ said:
⟨And verily, this is My Straight Path, so follow it, and do not follow other paths, for they will separate you away from His Path⟩⁴

The Right Path of Allah ﷻ is the one followed by His Prophet ﷺ and the Companions ﷺ; He ﷻ said:
⟨Yā-Sīn. By the Qur'an, full of wisdom. Truly you are one of the Messengers, on the Straight Path⟩⁵,

---

¹ Surah Al-A'raf, verse 16-17.
² Surah Fatir, verse 6.
³ Surah Al-A'raf, verse 27.
⁴ Surah Al-An'am, verse 153.
⁵ Surah Yā-Sīin, verse 1.

# The Whispering of the Shaytan

❴Verily, you indeed are on the straight guidance❵[1],

❴You are indeed guiding to the Straight Path❵[2]

So, whoever follows the Path of the Prophet ﷺ is on the Right Path, and is among those whom Allah ﷻ loves and forgives their sins. And whoever diverges from the actions and words of the Prophet ﷺ is an innovator, a follower of the Path of Satan, and not among those whom Allah ﷻ has promised Rewards and Mercy.

People who are under the influence of Satan's whisperings are likely to obey his commands, and reject the Sunnah of the Prophet ﷺ and his Companions ﷢. Their blind obedience to Satan leads some of them to believe that if they perform *wudu'* and *Salaah* in the manner of the Prophet ﷺ, their *wudu'* and *Salaah* would be invalid.

They also believe that feeding the children in the way of the Prophet ﷺ, and eating together, in a group, from one plate (the way Muslims eat their meals in general), would contaminate the meal, making it impure.

Satan's control over such people has led them to obey him blindly. It is similar to the school of the Sophists who deny the facts of the creation and things which are perceptible through senses. They even disclaim man's

---

[1] Surah Al-Hajj, verse 67.
[2] Surah Ash-Shura, verse 52.

# The Whispering of the Shaytan

knowledge about himself, in matters of certainty and necessity. Such people wash themselves, recite with their tongues, listen with their own ears, yet still have doubt about their actions; whether they have actually done any of them or not! Satan makes them even doubt their own intentions, which they certainly know, deep in their hearts. Instead, they accept Satan's whispering, that they have not made the intention for *Salaah* for example, to argue against their own certainty. It is all an exaggeration in their obedience to Satan, and acceptance of his *waswasah*; so whoever reaches this level of obedience to Satan has achieved complete obedience to him.

A person under Satan's whisperings accepts the devil's words, harming himself/herself, sometimes by plunging himself/herself in cold water, or by opening his eyes under cold water, washing them until they become sore.

Abu Al-Faraj bin Al-Juziy reported from Abu Al-Wafa' bin 'Uqayl that a man said to him: "I dip in water many times, and still have doubt whether I have washed properly or not, so what is your opinion?" The Shaikh said to him: "Go, for the obligation of *Salaah* is withdrawn from you." He said: "Why do you say so?" The Shaikh replied: "Because the Prophet ﷺ said: 'There are three persons whose actions are not recorded: a lunatic whose mind is deranged till he is restored to consciousness, a sleeper till he awakes, and a boy till he

# The Whispering of the Shaytan

reaches puberty'[1] and whoever dips in water many times, yet still has doubt whether he is wet or not, is a lunatic."

Ibn Qudaamah added: "Satan occupies the minds of such people until they miss the time for performing *Salaah* in congregation, or keeps them busy with making the "*niyyah*" (intention) until they miss the time of the First *Takbeer* (the saying of the first *Allahu Akbar* after the Imam, at the beginning of the *Salaah*), or even miss a whole *Rak'ah* or more.

It was reported to me that a man, who was under strong influence from Satan's whisperings, was extremely obsessed and concerned about expressing his *niyyah* before performing any *Salaah*; one day, he kept on repeating the word "I pray" many times, and "*Salaah* of such and such."

Satan has indeed managed to torment some people in this world before they reach the Hereafter; he has taken them away from following the Sunnah of the Prophet ﷺ, such that they have become people of extreme and excessive practices in religion, while they think that they are doing good.

Whoever wants to rid himself from this trial has to believe, with certainty, that the truth is in following the Sunnah of the Prophet ﷺ, in both his words and actions. One has to be certain that one is on the Right Path, and

---

[1] Recorded by Ahmad and Abu Dawud, on the authority of Ali and 'Umar ؓ, and it is Sahih.

## The Whispering of the Shaytan

that any other path is but an enticement from Satan, in the form of his devilish whisperings. One has to know for certain that Satan is his clear enemy, who only entices one to evil deeds; as Allah ﷻ said:
⟨**he only invites his followers that they may become the dwellers of the blazing fire**⟩[1].

He should give up anything that opposes the Sunnah of the Prophet ﷺ, and have no doubt that the Prophet ﷺ was certainly on the Right Path, and that whoever should doubt such a fact would indeed become a non-Muslim, and a disbeliever. One should look at the manner the Companions and the Tabi'in (followers who came after the Companions) who followed the Prophet ﷺ in his Sunnah, and should imitate them; for one of them said: "There were people (Companions) before me, whom if they did not wash beyond their nails, I would not have washed beyond them;" that was Ibrahim An-Nakha'i.

Zin Al-'Abidin once said to his son: "O son, get me some clothing to wear when I respond to the call of nature; for I have seen flies landing on filth, then touch clothing afterwards. Then, he observed taht neither the Prophet ﷺ nor his Companions used to wear more than two pieces of clothing, so he cancelled his request.

Whenever 'Umar bin Al-Khattab ؓ was determined to do something, and then was told that the Prophet ﷺ never did such a thing, he would abandon the idea. Once, he said:

---
[1] Surah Faṭir, verse 6.

# The Whispering of the Shaytan

"I am considering giving up wearing this clothing, as I heard that they are painted with the urine of old people!" then Ubay ؓ asked him: "Why are you giving it up? For the Prophet ﷺ used to wear it, and his contemporaries, and had Allah ﷻ known that it was unlawful, He ﷻ would have made it clear to His Prophet ﷺ." So 'Umar ؓ replied: "You are right."

One should know that none of the Companions were under the influence of *Waswasah*, for if the latter (*waswasah*) were a virtue, Allah ﷻ would not conceal it from His Prophet ﷺ and the Companions ؓ, who are the most preferred creation to Allah ﷻ. If the Prophet ﷺ had lived in this time he ﷺ would have loathed them, and if they had lived in the time of 'Umar ؓ, he would have punished them.

I hereby mention the diversity in their belief or teachings in details:

# The Whispering of the Shaytan

## *Niyyah* in *Taharah* and *Salaah*

*Niyyah* is the intention and will to do an activity. Its place is in the heart, as it is unrelated to the tongue. Therefore, it was reported from the Prophet ﷺ and his Companions ؓ that they used to make a *niyyah* for each circumstance. These expressions[1], which were invented to be used at the beginning of *wudu'* and *Salaah*, have been made the subject of dispute among people under Satan's influence. He always reminds them to pronounce those expressions properly, and so you find one of them repeating the words of *niyyah* with difficulty, while this is not part of *Salaah* at all; rather the *niyyah* is the intention in the heart to do an act. Whoever sits down to perform wudu' has indeed made *niyyah* to do *wudu'*; and whoever stands up to perform *Salaah* has indeed made the *niyyah* to do *Salaah*.

Therefore, one's *niyyah* is made, automatically, with any intended activity; it does not need any effort, and if one tried to free one's chosen activities, one would not be able to do so. If Allah ﷻ had charged His servants to perform *wudu'* and *Salaah* without any *niyyah*, He ﷻ would have charged them above their ability. If a person has any doubts about not having a *niyyah* (to do something) then this could be seen as a sign of lunacy, because a person's knowledge about himself is

---
[1] Expressions such as: "I intend to perform *wudu'* for such and such a *Salaah*," etc.

# The Whispering of the Shaytan

considered a matter of normality; so how could a sane person have doubts about his actions?

When a person stands up to perform *Salaat adh-Dhuhr* (noon prayer), for example, behind the Imam, how could he have any doubt about performing such an act? If anyone should ask him about a different matter, he would certainly reply: "I am busy, I am about to perform *Salaat adh-Dhuhr*."

What is more amazing to me than all this is the fact that the other people around him would surely know what his intention was from the situation. If a man was seen sitting in a row of people gathering at the time of *Salaah*, people would surely know that he was also waiting to perform *Salaah*. And if they had seen him stand up at the time of *Iqamah*[1], as the other people around him also stood up for it, they would know that he stood up to pray. If he moved forward to stand in front of them, people would know that he was their *imam* for that *Salaah*.

Therefore, if other people know his inner *niyyah* by his outer state; how could he deny it about himself? His acceptance of Satan's whisperings, that he never makes any *niyyah* (before any act), is an act of belief in the devil, a denial of true facts, a deviation from the Book of Allah and the *Sunnah* of His Prophet ﷺ, and from the path of the Companions ﷺ.

---
[1] The second call to the *Salaah*.

# The Whispering of the Shaytan

It is strange that one should have such doubts about one's *niyyah*, when one is about to start *Salaah*, while the Imam is in the position of *ruku'*[1]; if he feared missing a *Rak'ah*, he would certainly make *takbeer* quickly and join the Imam in that position. If one does not make one's *niyyah* throughout the standing position, when his mind is free, how could he make it in the short time that his mind is busy thinking about not missing the *Rak'ah*?

How was it that the Prophet ﷺ, and all his Companions and followers, never paid any attention to it? How was it only noticed by the one whose mind was under the influence of Satan? Does such a person believe, with his ignorance, that the devil is good advisor? Does he not know that the devil never calls or leads to anything good? What would such a person say about the *Salaah* of the Prophet ﷺ, and all the Muslims who did not act like him; that it is incomplete?

If such a person says: "This is an ailment that I suffer from." We would say: "Yes, and the reason for that is your acceptance of Satan's whisperings, and Allah does not forgive such deviation from the Sunnah. Can you not see that it was because Adam and Eve ﷺ accepted the whisperings of the devil once that they were expelled from Paradise, and they were eventually forgiven, as they were duly close to forgiveness; because there were none before them to act as an example to follow; while you have heard of, and Allah ﷻ has warned you against the

---
[1] A bending of the torso from an upright position, followed by two prostrations in *Salaah*.

## The Whispering of the Shaytan

trial and temptations of the devil. Allah ﷻ has shown you the enmity of Satan, and the Right Path to follow; therefore, you have no excuse to deviate from the Sunnah of His Prophet ﷺ."

Shaikh Ibn Taymiyyah said: "There are among such people who come with ten innovations which were never practised by the Prophet ﷺ nor any of his Companions. They say, for example: *'a'udhu billahi mina shaytani rajeem* (I seek refuge in Allah from Satan, the accursed). I intend to pray *Salaat adh-Dhuhr* in its due time, fulfilling the Command of Allah, four *raka'at*, facing the *Qiblah*.' Then, he would shake his body and lower his head, and scream "*Allahu Akbar*", as if saying *takbeer* (Allah Akbar) to the enemy."

One of the aspects of *waswasah*, which corrupts one's *Salaah*, is the repetition of a letter in a particular word; such as when pronouncing *takbeer*: '*takkk, takkk*,' and in *tahiyyat*: '*tahiy, tahiy...*' These visible aspects can be a factor to invalidate one's *Salaah*, and if the person is an Imam, leading other people, he may corrupt their *Salaah* as well. In this case, *Salaah* which is the greatest act of worship could be distancing such a person from Allah ﷻ more than a major sin. Any other aspect that does not lead to wholly corrupting one's *Salaah* is considered *makrooh* (disliked and reprehensible), because it is a deviation from the Sunnah of the Prophet ﷺ.

Such a person, under the effect of extreme *waswasah*, may also raise his voice, and entice others to speak ill of

# The Whispering of the Shaytan

him. Therefore, he has gathered upon himself all the wrong doing: obedience to Satan, differing from the Sunnah, committing innovations in worship, torturing himself and wasting time, keeping himself busy with what reduces the reward from Allah ﷻ and missing what is beneficial, exposing himself to slandering, and tempting the ignorant to follow him; saying that if such a thing was not beneficial, he would not have done it; as if the Sunnah was incomplete.

Abu Hamid Al-Ghazali and others have said: "The cause of *waswasah* is either ignorance of Shar' (Islam) or insanity; and both of which are major defects."

Muslim reported in his Sahih book, on the authority of 'Uthman bin Al-'As who said: "I said: 'O Messenger of Allah, Satan intervenes between me and my prayer and he confounds me.' Thereupon, the Prophet ﷺ said: 'That is the doing of the Satan who is known as khinzab; when you perceive its effect, seek refuge with Allah from it, and spit three times to your left.' I did that and Allah ﷻ dispelled that from me."[1]

Therefore, people under the effect of *waswasah* are a joy and delight for Khinzab and his companions to behold. We seek refuge in Allah ﷻ from them.

---

[1] Recorded by Muslim.

# The Whispering of the Shaytan

## Excessive use of water in wudu' and bathing

Ahmad reported in his "Musnad", on the authority of Abdullah bin 'Amru that the Prophet ﷺ passed by Sa'd, as he was performing ablution, and said: "Do not be wasteful." Sa'd ؓ said: "Is there even wastefulness with water?" He ﷺ replied: "Yes, even if you were performing ablution from a flowing river."[1]

Ubay bin Ka'b ؓ reported that the Prophet ﷺ said: "There is a Satan for ablution called 'Al-Walhan', so be on your guard against the evil promptings of (wasting) water."[2]

A desert Arab came to the Messenger of Allah ﷺ and asked about ablution. He ﷺ demonstrated (washing each part of his body) thrice, and then said: "That is the method of the ablution, and he who does more than this has done wrong, transgressed the limit, and oppressed himself."[3]

Umm Sa'd ؓ reported that the Prophet ﷺ said: "A *Saa'* (a measure) used to be equal to a *Mudd* (another kind of measure), which is a third of the Mudd that we use today; but the *Saa'* of today has become too large. One *Mudd* of water is enough for *wudu'*, and a *Saa'* is enough for

---
[1] Recorded by Ahmad.
[2] Recorded by At-Tirmidhi.
[3] Recorded by At-Tirmidhi, Abu Dawud, Ibn Maajah and An-Nassai.

# The Whispering of the Shaytan

making *Ghusl* (taking a bath). There will be people who will exceed this, and so would be opposing my Sunnah. But those who adopt my Sunnah (in their life) would be in the Garden of Eden."

It was also reported in Sunan Al-Athram, on the authority of Salim bin Abu Al-Ja'd from Jabir bin Abdullah who said: "A Mudd is enough for *wudu'*, while a *Saa'* is enough for performing *ghusl* from *janabah*." A man said: 'It would not be enough for me.' Thereupon, Jabir became so furious and said: 'It was enough for someone who was better than you, and more hairy."

'Aishah reported that she and the Prophet used to perform ablution from one container of three *Mudds*, or thereabouts."[1]

Habib Al-Ansari reported: "I heard 'Abbad bin Tamim who reported, on the authority of my grand-mother, Umm Umarah, saying: 'The Prophet wanted to perform ablution. A vessel containing 2/3 *Mudd* of water was brought to him.'"[2]

Ibrahim An-Nakha'i said: "The Companions were more mindful of not wasting water than you; they regarded a third of *Mudd* of water as enough for ablution."

---

[1] Recorded by Muslim.
[2] Recorded by Abu Dawud and An-Nassai.

# The Whispering of the Shaytan

This is a great exaggeration; as a *Mudd* of water is a very small quantity indeed.

Anas bin Malik ؓ said: "The Prophet ﷺ used to perform ablution with a *Mudd* of water, and *ghusl* with one *Saa'*, equivalent to three *Mudds* of water."[1]

Safinah ؓ said: "The Messenger of Allah ﷺ took a bath with one *Saa'* of water (after sexual intercourse) and performed ablution with one *Mudd*."[2]

Al-Qasim bin Muhammad bin Abu Bakr ؓ performed ablution with half a *Mudd* of water, or a little more than that."

Muhammad bin 'Ajlan said: "Adequate knowledge of the *Deen* of Allah ﷻ is knowing how to perform *wudu'* properly, using little water."

Abdullah bin Mughaffal ؓ said: "I heard the Prophet ﷺ say: In this community, there will be some people who will exceed the limits, in purification as well as in supplication."[3]

Therefore, if you compare this Hadith with Allah's Words in this Verse:
⟨**Verily, Allah does not love the transgressors**⟩,

---

[1] Recorded Al-Bukhari and Muslim.
[2] Recorded by Muslim.
[3] Recorded by Abu Dawud.

# The Whispering of the Shaytan

you would know that Allah ﷻ loves to see His Servants worshipping Him, and you would understand that the ablution of the person under the effect of *waswasah* is not an act of worship accepted by Allah ﷻ.

The corrupting aspect of *waswasah* is that it occupies the person under its influence to use more water than he needs, especially if it is the property of others, as in a public bath.

## Disregarding any *waswasah* about breaking wudu'

Abu Hurayrah ؓ reported that the Prophet ﷺ said: "If any of you has a pain in his abdomen, but is doubtful whether or not anything has issued of him, he should not leave the mosque to make wudu' unless he hears a sound or perceives a smell."[1]

Abdullah bin Zayd ؓ said: "It was reported to the Prophet ﷺ that a man imagined to have passed wind during prayer. He ﷺ said: 'He should not leave his prayer unless he hears a sound or smells something.'"[2]

Abu Sa'id Al-Khudri ؓ reported that the Prophet ﷺ said: "The devil may approach one of you during his *Salaah*,

---
[1] Recorded by Muslim.
[2] Recorded by Al-Bukhari and Muslim.

# The Whispering of the Shaytan

and pull a hair from your back. If the man were to imagine that his ablution had been broken, he should not leave his prayer, unless he should hear a sound or perceive a smell."[1]

The Prophet ﷺ also said: "If the devil comes to one of you in his prayer, and tells you: 'You have been defiled', he should say: 'You have told a lie,' except when he senses a smell with his nose, or a sound with his ears."

Shaikh Abu Muhammad bin Qudamah Al-Maqdisi said: "It is recommended to sprinkle one's private part and trousers with water after urinating (in the toilet), in order to prevent any *waswasah*. And so, if one finds any wetness in his clothing, he would say: "This is the water that I sprinkled there." Al-Hakam bin Sufyan At-Thaqafi ؓ reported that when the Prophet ﷺ urinated, he performed ablution and sprinkled water on his private parts."[2]

---

[1] Recorded by Abu Dawud.
[2] Recorded by Abu Dawud.

# The Whispering of the Shaytan

## Things that people are harsh in implementing, while the Prophet ﷺ was indulgent towards himself with them

Many people practise methods of cleaning, after urinating, which are signs of extreme *waswasah*:

They would hold their private part, cough to expel any wine left inside, walk few steps or even jump up and sit down immediately. They would check to see if there is something left behind, or even pour more water and then cover it with a piece of cloth. All this because they were suspicious that there might be a few drops of urine left inside, which could later defile their wudu'!

Shaikh Ibn Taymiyyah said that this is all aspects of *waswasah* and innovation in religion; and I have asked him about a *Gharib* Hadith – which is not confirmed – on the authority of 'Isa bin Dawud, from his father who said: "The Prophet ﷺ said: 'When one of you urinates, he should wipe his private part three times"[1] But he replied that it was not valid. He also added: "Had it been a way of the Prophet ﷺ, the Companions would have been the first to adopt the example. In fact, a Jew said to Salman Al-Farisi: 'Your Prophet has taught you everything, even about excrement,' to which he replied: 'Yes, He has forbidden us to face the *Qiblah* at

---

[1] Recorded by Imam Ahmad and Abu Dawud, and it was said to be one of the weak Hadiths by Al-Albani (1621).

the time of easing or urinating, to clean with right hand, and to clean with less than three stones, or clean with dung or bone.'[1]

## Some acts that show someone to be an innovator in religion

There are some acts which the Prophet ﷺ has considered lightly for his Ummah, while some people have focused on them too much, such as:

Walking with bare feet on the roads, then performing *Salaah* without washing them. Abu Dawud reported in his Sunan that a woman from the tribe of Abd Al-Ash'hal said: "I said: 'O Messenger of Allah, I walk through a dirty place on my way to the mosque; what should I do?' he ﷺ said: 'Is there not a clean place after that dirty one?' she replied: 'Yes,' he then said: 'What comes after it would clean it.'[2]

Abdullah bin Mas'ud ؓ said: "We did not perform ablution after treading on anything."[3]

---

[1] Recorded by Muslim, Abu Dawud and At-Tirmidhi.
[2] Recorded by Abu Dawud and At-Tirmidhi.
[3] Recorded by Abu Dawud and At-Tirmidhi.

# The Whispering of the Shaytan

Ali bin Abi Talib ؓ reported that he had walked through muddy water, then he ؓ entered the mosque and performed *Salaah* without washing his feet."

Ibn 'Abbas ؓ was asked about someone who steps on something impure, to which he ؓ replied: "If someone steps on something dry, it has no effect on his *wudu'*, but if he steps one step on something wet or damp, then he should wash the place affected."

Hafs bin 'Affan Al-Hanafi Al-Yamani said: "I walked with Abdullah bin 'Umar ؓ to the mosque, and when we reached it, I decided to go to the *wudu'* area to wash my feet, but he said to me: 'You do not need to wash them; for you stepped on a dirty spot, then you stepped on a clean spot after it, so your feet become clean again.' So we entered the mosque together and performed *Salaah*."

Abu Ash-Sha'ta' said: "Ibn 'Umar ؓ used to walk bare footed in Mina through areas covered in dry blood, then he would enter the mosque and perform *Salaah*, without washing his feet."

'Imran bin Hudayr said: "I used to walk to the Friday Prayers with Abu Mujliz, and on the road, there were some unclean spots, but he used to step on them saying: These are only dry black spots.' He walked into the mosque with bare feet, and performed *Salaah*, without washing them."

# The Whispering of the Shaytan

## The way to perform *Salaah* in shoes

If one's socks or shoes are affected by an impurity, it is lawful to wipe them against the ground completely, and then perform *Salaah*, as it was reported in the authentic Sunnah:

Abu Hurayrah reported that the Prophet said: "If any of you steps on something impure, then dust or earth is a substance he can use to purify it."[1]

Abu Sa'id Al-Khudri said: "While the Messenger of Allah was leading his Companions in prayer, he took off his sandals and laid them on his left side; when the people saw this, they removed their sandals. When the Messenger of Allah finished his prayer, he asked: 'What made you remove your sandals?' They replied: 'We saw you remove your sandals, so we removed our sandals.' The Messenger of Allah then said: 'Gabriel came to me and informed me that there was dirt on them. When any of you comes to the mosque, he should check; if he finds dirt on his sandals, he should wipe it off and pray in them.'"[2]

The same applies to the long clothes of women; for a woman asked Umm Salamah : "I am a woman who wears long dresses, and I have to walk through a dirty place; so what should I do?' Umm Salamah replied:

---
[1] Recorded by Abu Dawud.
[2] Recorded by Abu Dawud.

# The Whispering of the Shaytan

'The Messenger of Allah ﷺ said: What comes after it would clean it.'[1]

The Prophet ﷺ allowed women to loosen their clothing, even though it might touch dirty places, but did not command them to wash them immediately. Instead, he ﷺ told them that the dust of the earth purifies any thing affected by dirty ground.

## Performing *Salaah* with shoes on

People under the influence of Satan's whisperings do not see it appropriate (or even comfortable) to perform *Salaah* with their shoes on, in some circumstances, even though the Prophet ﷺ had done so, and commanded his Companions ﷺ to do likewise.

Anas bin Malik ﷺ reported that the Prophet ﷺ performed *Salaah* with his shoes on.[2]

Shaddad bin Aws reported that the Prophet ﷺ said: "Act differently from the Jews; for they do not perform *Salaah* in their sandals or shoes."[3]

---

[1] Recorded by Abu Dawud.
[2] Recorded by Al-Bukhari and Muslim.
[3] Recorded by Abu Dawud.

# The Whispering of the Shaytan

Imam Ahmad was asked: "Can a man pray in his shoes?" he replied: "Yes, by Allah!"

Abu Sa'id Al-Khudri ﷺ said: "If one of you comes to the mosque, he should check his shoes; if they are dirty, he should wipe them, then perform *Salaah* wearing them."[1]

## It is the Sunnah of the Prophet ﷺ to perform *Salaah* wherever he was

The Prophet ﷺ used to perform *Salaah* wherever he was, at every place, except forbidden places, such as: cemeteries, toilets or bathrooms, and resting places of camels. He ﷺ said: "The earth has been made for me (and my followers) a place for praying and something with which to perform *Tayammum*. Therefore, my followers can pray anywhere and whenever the time for prayers is due."[2] He ﷺ would perform *Salaah* in cattle pen sometimes.

Ibn Al-Mundhir said: "All the scholars have agreed that it is lawful to perform *Salaah* in cattle pens, except Ash-Safi'i, who said: "I dislike such a matter, except if the pen was free from animal dung.

---

[1] Hadith Sahih reported by Shaikh Al-Albani in his book: "Irwa' Al-Ghalil".
[2] Recorded by Al-Bukhari.

# The Whispering of the Shaytan

Abu Hurayrah ؓ reported that the Prophet ﷺ said: "Observe prayers in sheep folds, but not in camel folds."[1]

Imam Ahmad reported a Hadith of Abdullah bin Al-Mughaffal who said: "The Prophet ﷺ said: 'Observe *Salaah* in sheep folds, but not in camel folds; for they are created by demons."

The same Hadith was also reported by Jabir bin Samurrah Al-Barra' bin 'Azib, Usayd bin Al-Hudayr, Dhee Al-'Izzah, and Anas bin Malik ؓ, and recorded by Al-Bukhari, Muslim, Abu Dawud, An-Nassai, Ibn Maajah, At-Tabarani and Ahmad; all their narrators were trustworthy.

The Prophet ﷺ said: "The whole earth is a place to pray, except for a cemetery or bathroom."[2] So where is the guidance of suspicious people who perform *Salaah* only on prayer mats, spread over the carpet?

Such people rightly deserve the saying of Ibn Mas'ud ؓ: "Either you are more rightly guided than the Companions of Muhammad ﷺ, or you are indeed misguided."[3]

---

[1] Hadith Sahih, recorded by At-Tirmidhi.
[2] Reported by all the scholars with the Sunan books, except An-Nassai.
[3] Ibn Mas'ud ؓ mentioned these words about some people who gathered inside the mosque, in a session led by a man who would ask them to say *Takbeer* (Allah *Akbar*) or *Tahleel* (*la Ilaha Illallah*) or *Tasbeeh* (*Subhanallah*) a hundred times, and the Hadith was transmitted by Darami (1/68).

# The Whispering of the Shaytan

## The Companions of the Prophet ﷺ used to walk barefooted to the mosque

Yahya bin Watthab said: "I asked Ibn 'Abbas: 'Can a man perform ablution, then walk barefooted to the mosque?' He ؓ replied: 'Yes, there is no harm in that.'

Kamal bin Ziyad said: "I saw Ali bin Abi Talib ؓ walk in pouring rain, then enter the mosque and perform *Salaah*, without washing his feet."

Ibrahim An-Nakha'i said: "The Companions of the Prophet ﷺ used to walk in rain (on wet clay), enter the mosque and perform *Salaah*."

Ibn Al-Mundhir said: "Ibn 'Umar ؓ walked barefooted in Mina, then performed *Salaah*, without making *wudu'* again." He added: "And those who adopted such an opinion were: 'Alqamah, Al-Aswad, Abdullah bin Al-Mughaffal, Sa'id bin Al-Musayyib, Ash-Sha'abi, Imam Ahmad, Abu Haneefah, Imam Malik, and some from the Shafi'i school. This is the opinion of the majority of scholars; because had it been considered as a cancellation of wudu', it would have become a great burden upon the worshippers, against the objectives of Islam; just like the case of the food of the disbelievers and their clothing."

Abu Al-Barakat, Ibn Taymiyyah said: "All this strengthens the purity of the earth when it dries up; because people still come across filth in paths which they

# The Whispering of the Shaytan

frequently use, such as the way to the market or to the mosque, etc; and if they are not pure after being dry, then they would have to avoid walking on them, and it would no have been lawful for them to walk in bare feet.

The Prophet ﷺ used to order people to wipe their sandals against the earth if they saw something on them, before entering the mosque. So, if this action caused the earth to become impure, he ﷺ would not have told them to do so, because other people came barefooted.

This is the opinion of sheikh Ibn Taymiyyah; while Abu Qilabah said: "The dryness of the earth is its purity."

## What is the Sunnah for when *Madhiy*[1] touches one's clothes?

Sahl bin Hunayf ؓ felt distressed about frequent flowing of *madhiy*, so he ؓ asked the Prophet ﷺ, who answered: "Ablution will be sufficient for you for this." He ؓ added: "What should I do if it smears my clothes?" he ﷺ replied: "Take a handful of water and sprinkle it on your clothes, if you find it left a smear."[2]

---

[1] Prostatic fluid.
[2] Recorded by Abu Dawud.

# The Whispering of the Shaytan

So he ﷺ authorised his people to sprinkle water over the spot affected with any dirt, the way we purify our clothes if they become wet with a baby's urine[1].

Shaikh Ibn Taymiyyah said: "This is the correct opinion; because such an impurity (*madhiy*) is hard to prevent, because of its frequent occurrence for a young single man.

## Using stones for purification[2], and the ruling regarding pus

All the scholars are in agreement concerning the Sunnah of the Prophet ﷺ of using stones to purify oneself (after answering the call of nature), both in winter and summer; despite the fact that the area becomes sweaty, and it may sprinkle on the inside of one's clothing; yet he ﷺ never ordered for it to be washed.

Also exempted from any sort of purification are touching certain animal droppings, such as that of horses, donkeys and lions; as detailed in a narration reported by Imam

---

[1] Umm Qays bint Muhsin reported that she came to the Prophet ﷺ with her baby, who urinated on the Prophet's clothes; he ﷺ asked for some water and sprinkled it over the affected area of his clothes, but did not wash it out completely. (Recorded by Al-Bukhari, Muslim, and the four scholars of Sunan books.

[2] Purification after the call of nature.

# The Whispering of the Shaytan

Ahmad. It was approved by Shaikh Ibn Taymiyyah, because of the difficulty in avoiding them.

Al-Waleed bin Muslim said: "I said to Al-Awza'i: 'What about the urine of animals whose meat are prohibited?' he replied: 'The Companions used to be affected by that during their invasions; yet they never washed it off their bodies or clothes.'"

Imam Ahmad and Sheikh Ibn Taymiyyah both state that it is not necessary to clean any marks of pus on body or clothes, because there is no proof for declaring it impure. Some scholars, like Abu Barakaat, claim that pus is pure; while Ibn 'Umar never stopped his prayer when he saw pus in his body, as was the case with blood.

Abu Mijlaz was aked about when pus could affect one's body or clothes, to which he replied: "It is not impure; for Allah ﷻ mentioned blood (as impure), but did not mention pus."

Is'haq bin Raahawayh said: "I consider everything, including dirt, which does not require ablution, to be pleasant, except blood."

Imam Ahmad was asked: "Are blood and pus the same according to your judgment?" He replied: "No, people never differed regarding blood, but they did regarding pus." And he added: "I consider pus not to be as impure as blood."

# The Whispering of the Shaytan

Abu Haneefah said: "If a mouse's droppings fall into some wheat and got milled with it, or got mixed with flowing fat, it is lawful to eat it as long as it does not alter its state. But if it falls into water, then it would become impure.

A companion of Ash-Shafi'i stated that it is even legal to eat wheat affected by donkeys' urine when threshing it, without washing it, and added that the pious predecessors (The Companions of the Prophet ﷺ) were not too cautious about it.

Aishah, may Allah be pleased with her, said: "We used to eat meat, while streak of blood (which dripped from the meat) still remained on the pot."

Allah ﷻ has permitted the eating of animals chased and caught by hunting dogs, but did not order the washing of the mark of the dog's mouth; neither did the Prophet ﷺ, nor any of the companions ﷺ.

Many scholars among the Companions ﷺ and the followers, such as Abdullah bin 'Umar, 'Ata' bin Abi Rabah, Sa'id bin Al-Mussayyib, Tawus, Salim, Mujahid, Ash-Sha'bi, Ibrahim An-Nakha'i, Az-Zuhari, Yahya bin Sa'id Al-Ansari, Al-Hakam, Al-Awza'i, Malik bin Anas Is'haq bin Raahawayh, Abu Thawr and Imam Ahmad; they all declared that if a person notices a dirty mark or stain on one's body or clothes after *Salaah*, but was not aware of it, or knew of it but forgot it, or was unable to remove it, then one's *Salaah* is still valid, and one does not have to redo it."

## Carrying Children during *Salaah*

The Prophet ﷺ led *Salaah* while carrying his granddaughter Umamah, daughter of Zaynab ﷺ. As he bowed, he would put her down, picking her up again, as he got up.

He ﷺ kept on doing this until he had finished *Salaah*."[1]

It is a proof of the lawfulness of performing *Salaah* in the clothes of a nurse, a breastfeeding mother, or a menstruating woman, and with a child, as long as their impurity is not certain.

Abu Hurayrah ﷺ said: "We were performing *Salaah* 'Isha' with the Prophet ﷺ; when he ﷺ prostrated, Al-Hasan and Al-Husayn jumped on his back, and when he raised his head, he ﷺ picked them up gently from his back and put them in front of him. He did that until he had finished *Salaah*."[2]

Shidad bin Al-Had reported from his father: "The Prophet ﷺ came out to us carrying Al-Hasan or Al-Husayn; he ﷺ

---

[1] Recorded by Al-Bukhari and Muslim.
[2] Recorded by Imam Ahmad.

put him down, and made the *Takbeer* so as to lead us in *Salaah*. During *Salaah* he made one long prostration, then after he had finished, he ﷺ said: 'My son got on my back, so I did not want to rush to put him down.'[1]

'Aishah, may Allah be pleased with her, said: "The Messenger of Allah ﷺ and I used to lie under one cloth at night, even while I was menstruating. If anything from me smeared him, he washed the same place (that was smeared), but did not wash beyond it. If anything from him smeared his clothes, he washed the same place, but did not wash beyond that, and even prayed with it (i.e. in the same clothes)."[2]

'Aishah also reported: "I would drink when I was menstruating, then I would hand it to the Messenger of Allah ﷺ, and he would put his mouth where mine had been, and drink."[3]

## The Polytheists' Clothes

The Prophet ﷺ wore clothes made by the polytheists when performing *Salaah*.

---

[1] Recorded by Imam Ahmad and An-Nassai.
[2] Recorded by Abu Dawud.
[3] Recorded by Muslim.

# The Whispering of the Shaytan

'Umar bin Al-Khattab was worried about wearing clothes which were dyed with urine; so Ubay bin Malik said to him: "Why have you forbidden yourself from wearing them? The Prophet ﷺ wore them, and it was worn by his contemporaries. If it was unlawful to wear then Allah ﷻ would have revealed it to His Messenger." 'Umar ؓ replied: "You are right."

Once an infant was brought to the Prophet ﷺ (to invoke Allah's blessings upon it) however, it urinated on his clothes. He ﷺ just asked for water and poured it over the place of the urine, but did not wash his clothes.

When 'Umar bin Al-Khattab ؓ came to Al-Jaabiyah, he ؓ borrowed a piece of clothe from a Christian and put it on, until they washed his own clothes. He ؓ also performed ablution using a container that belonged to a Christian.

Salman Al-Farisi and Abu Darda' ؓ performed *Salaah* in a house of a Christian woman. Abu Darda' ؓ asked her: "Is there a pure place in your house in which we can perform *Salaah*?" She replied: "Purify your heart, and pray in any place you like in my house." Salman ؓ then told him: "Accept her words."

# The Whispering of the Shaytan

## The use of water left in open containers

The Companions and the Followers ﷺ used to perform ablution from open containers, yet never asked whether they were impure or not (whether they had been touched by a dog or a lion, etc).

Yahya bin Sa'id ﷺ said: "Umar bin Al-Khattab ﷺ set out with a group that included 'Amru bin Al-'As ﷺ. When they reached a pond, 'Amru asked its owner: 'Do lions (or wild animals) drink from your pond?' 'Umar ﷺ interrupted and told the man: 'You do not need to tell us; for lions drink from our water and we drink from theirs.'"[1]

The Prophet ﷺ was asked: "Can we perform ablution from water left by asses?" He ﷺ replied: "Yes, and also water left by lions (or wild animals)."[2]

If something is dropped into water and one is uncertain whether it is water or urine, he should not inquire about it. If a person is asked about it, he should not answer, even if he knows that the liquid dropped in water is impure; so it need not be washed.

'Umar bin Al-Khattab ﷺ was once walking with one of his companions, and something was dropped on him. His companion asked the people: 'Is your water pure?' 'Umar

---
[1] Recorded by Imam Malik in Al-Muwatta'.
[2] Recorded by Ibn Maajah.

# The Whispering of the Shaytan

🙏 interrupted, saying: 'O people, do not tell us (if it is pure or not)' and walked away.¹

Skaikh Ibn Taymiyyah said: "Likewise, if anything soft touches one's feet or long clothing, and he does not know its nature; he should not try to find out what it is." 'Umar's example is best in this case.

This is the correct understanding of *fiqh*; for the rulings apply to the person after he knows its reasons and causes, otherwise amnesty applies. What has been forgiven by Allah ﷻ should not be inquired about.

## Performing *Salaah* with a little – but not flowing – blood

Al-Bukhari said: "Al-Hasan Al-Basri 🙏 said: 'Muslims may even perform *Salaah* with their wounds.'

He also said: "Ibn Umar 🙏 squeezed a wound and blood came out, yet he 🙏 did not renew his ablution. Ibn Abi Awfa spit blood and yet he pursued his *Salaah*. While 'Umar bin Al-Khattab performed *Salaah* while blood dripped from his wound."²

---
¹ Recorded by Imam Ahmad.
² This Hadith was on the authority of 'Umar bin Al-Khattab 🙏, and was not reported by Al-Bukhari among the Traditions in the chapter regarding those who judge the invalidity of *wudu'* only by the effects of the private parts. Al-Bukhari mentioned a Hadith of Jabir bin

# The Whispering of the Shaytan

## Breastfeeding women's clothes

Since the time of the Prophet ﷺ until now, breastfeeding women still perform *Salaah* in their normal clothes, even though their babies vomiting drip over their clothes and bodies, and they do not have to wash them; because the baby's saliva is pure for the benefit of its mouth, just as the cat's saliva is pure for its mouth.

The Prophet ﷺ said: "It is not unclean; it is one of those who moves around amongst you." He ﷺ once tilted a vessel of water for the cat until it drank some of it.[1]

Kabshah, daughter of Ka'b Ibn Malik and wife of Ibn Abu Qatadah, reported: "Abu Qatadah visited me, and I poured water for his ablution. A cat came and drank some of it and he tilted the vessel for it until it drank some of it. He saw me looking at him and asked me: 'Are you surprised, my niece?' I said: 'Yes.' He then reported the Messenger of Allah ﷺ as saying: 'It is not unclean; it is

---

Abdullah ؓ who said: "During the invasion of Dhat-Riqa', a watchman was hit with an arrow and continued his prayer even though he was bleeding." Al-Hafidh bin Hajar said that this Hadith was also recorded by Ahmad, Abu Dawud, Daraqutni, Ibn Khuzayma, Ibn Hibban and Al-Hakim. They all transmitted the Hadith on the authority of Ibn Ishaq, whose sheikh was trustworthy. He also added that it was clear that Al-Bukhari did not consider bleeding in *Salaah* as a cause to invalidate it; because he also mentioned the Hadith of Al-Hasan Al-Basri ؓ who said: "Muslims even perform *Salaah* with their wounds."

[1] Recorded Ahmad, Abu Dawud, Tirmidhi and Annassai.

## The Whispering of the Shaytan

one of those (males or females) who moves around amongst you.'"[1]

So the Prophet ﷺ used to perform ablution from water in which the cat drank, despite the fact that cats eat mice and other creatures.

The Companions ؓ and the followers used to perform *Salaah* while carrying their swords stained with blood; they simply used to wipe them.

Imam Ahmad defined the butcher's knife as pure; just by wiping it. He also stated that washing lines become clean if exposed to the sun after being used to hang impure clothing, and said that clean clothes can be hanged on them afterwards.

This is similar to the opinion of Abu Haneefah that the earth is purified by the wind and the sun, to the extent that it is lawful to be used for *Tayammum*.

Ibn 'Umar ؓ said: "Dogs used to enter and then urinate in the mosque, and the Companions never sprinkled any water in it". This is because the earth becomes pure by the wind and the sun.

The Sunnah of the Prophet ﷺ and his Companions states that water becomes unclean only when it changes (in colour or taste), even if it is of little quantity.

---

[1] Hadith Hasan Sahih, authenticated by Al-Bukhari, Al-'Uqayli, Ibn Khuzaymah and Ibn Hibban.

# The Whispering of the Shaytan

This is the opinion of the scholars in Al-Madinah and the majority of our pious predecessors. It was the opinion of 'Ata' bin Abu Rabah, Sa'id bin Al-Musayyib, Jabir bin Zayd, Al-Awza'i, Sufyan Ath-Thawri, Malik bin Anas, Abdurrahman bin Mahdi and Ibn Al-Mundhir. It was also the opinion of Ahmad and a group of my contemporary scholars, such as Ibn 'Uqayl, Our Shaikh Abu Al-'Abbas, and his Shaikh Ibn Abu 'Umar.

Ibn 'Abbas stated: "The Prophet said: 'Water is not defiled by anything.'"[1]

Abu Sa'id Al-Khudri said: "Some people asked the Prophet: 'Can we perform ablution out of the well of Buda'ah, which is a well into which menstrual clothes, dead dogs and stinking things were thrown?' he replied: 'Water is pure, and is not defiled by anything.'"[2]

In a Hadith reported by Abu Umamah, the Prophet said: "Water is pure and is not defiled by anything, except if something alters its smell, or taste or colour."[3]

Abu Sa'id Al-Khudri reported that the Prophet was asked about the purity of the ponds between Makkah and Madinah which were frequently used by lions, dogs and donkeys, to which he replied: "They are pure."

---
[1] Recorded by Imam Ahmad.
[2] Recorded by At-Tirmidhi who classified it as Hadith *Hasan*, and Imam Ahmad who classified it as Hadith Sahih.
[3] Recorded by Ibn Maajah.

# The Whispering of the Shaytan

Al-Bukhari said "Az-Zuhari said: 'There is no harm with the water as long as its taste, smell or colour are not changed."

## Accepting Food from the People of the Book

The Prophet ﷺ used to answer any invitation from the People of the Book, and would eat their meals.

A Jewish man invited him and offered him barley bread and fat. The Muslims used to eat the food of the People of the Book

'Umar bin Al-Khattab ؓ imposed on the People of the Book that they should invite any Muslim visitor (passerby), when he said: "Feed them from your own meals", as Allah ﷻ has made it lawful in the Qur'an.

When 'Umar ؓ came to Syria, the People of the Book made a meal for him and invited him. He ؓ said: "Where is it?" they said: "In the church." He disliked entering the church, but said to Ali ؓ: "Take the people in". Ali ؓ entered the church with the Muslims, and they all ate the meal offered. Ali ؓ started looking at the pictures on the wall of the church and said: "What if the Emir of the faithful had entered and ate here?"

## The similarity between Polytheism and forbidding what is lawful

Imam Ahmad reported that the Prophet ﷺ said: "I was sent with the *Hanifiyah* (true) *Samhah* (tolerant)" (i.e. Islam). So he ﷺ combined the fact that Islam is true and tolerant. It is true in its concept of the Oneness of Allah ﷻ, and tolerant in its practice (action). It is opposed to two things: polytheism and forbidding the lawful, which were both mentioned by the Prophet ﷺ in the Hadith Qudsi, in which Allah ﷻ said: "I have created My Servants pure; but devils came and led them astray from their religion (Islam), and forbade them to enjoy what I made lawful for them, and commanded them to join in worship with Me, which was unauthorised."

Polytheism and forbidding what is lawful are linked; Allah ﷻ censured the polytheists about them in Surat Al-An'am and Al-A'raf.

The Prophet ﷺ disliked narrow-mindedness in religion, and informed us of its futility when he ﷺ said: "Be on your guard against pettiness; for pettiness destroyed those

# The Whispering of the Shaytan

who were before you, as it incited them to shed blood and make lawful what was unlawful for them."[1]

Ibn Abu Shaybah ؓ said: "Abu Usamah reported that Mas'ar said: 'Ma'n bin Abdurrahman came to me with a book, and swore by Allah that it was written by his father. It was written in the book: 'Abdullah said: 'By Allah, for there is no god except Him; I have never met someone more severe on the petty-minded people (in religion) than the Prophet ﷺ."[2]

The Prophet ﷺ disliked the people who exceed the boundaries of his Sunnah (and those who practice his sunnah with extreme cautiousness); he said once, when he was observing *wisal*[3] fasting: "What about such people who observe uninterrupted fasts? By Allah, if the month were lengthened for me, I would have observed *wisal* fasting, so that those who act in an exaggerated manner would have been obliged to abandon their excesses."[4]

The Companions ؓ did not burden themselves with excessive acts of worship; they simply followed the best example, in that of the Prophet ﷺ; for Allah ﷻ said: ❨Say: No wage do I ask of you for this, nor am I one of *al-mukallifin* (those who pretend and fabricate things which do not exist)❩[5].

---

[1] Recorded by Muslim, on the authority of Jabir bin Abdullah ؓ.
[2] Recorded by Ibn Abu Shaybah.
[3] Uninterrupted fasting after the month of Ramadan.
[4] Recorded by Muslim, At-Tirmidhi and Abu Dawud.
[5] Surat Sād, verse 86.

# The Whispering of the Shaytan

Abdullah bin Mas'ud ﷺ said: "Whoever wants to follow the Sunnah should follow the Sunnah of those who died, because the living would always be subject to a *fitnah* (trial). Those (who died) were the Companions of Muhammad ﷺ; they were the best of this Ummah: they were more righteous, had more knowledge, and only worshiped Allah ﷻ with the Sunnah of His Prophet ﷺ. They were chosen by Allah ﷻ to accompany His Messenger, and establish His Religion. So, learn from their merits, and follow their footsteps; for they were on the Right Path."[1]

Anas bin Malik ﷺ said: "We were in the company of 'Umar ﷺ and he said: 'We were forbidden any excessive and unusual behaviour.'"

Malik bin Anas ﷺ reported that 'Umar bin Abdul-Aziz ﷺ said: 'The Prophet ﷺ and rulers after him enacted laws (Sunnah), and the implementation of this Sunnah is to believe in the Book of Allah (the Qur'an), and be completely devoted to the *Deen* of Allah ﷻ. One should not try to change it, nor seek an alternative, nor even study any laws which oppose it. Whoever follows it is rightly guided, and whoever seeks help from it is well supported, but whoever opposes it and follows other than the path of the believers, Allah ﷻ will guide him to Hell; the worst destination.

---

[1] Recorded by Imam Ahmad.

# The Whispering of the Shaytan

Malik ؓ reported that 'Umar ؓ said: "The Sunnah was prescribed for you, and obligations were decreed for you; you were left on a clear path, unless you should try to deviate people to the right or to the left."

This knowledge is carried by every successor of a righteous group, who denounce the corruption of extremists, the deviation of liars, and the interpretation of the ignorant.

The Prophet ﷺ informed us that corruption within Islam comes from such groups (mentioned above). Had Allah ﷻ not assigned people to defend His *Deen*, it would have been subjected to the same fate as the religions of previous Prophets.

## *Waswasah* in Pronouncing Letters

This is what the scholars said regarding this matter:
Abu Al-Faraj Al-Juzy said: "Iblis (Satan) confused some worshippers in their utterance of letters. You would find them sometimes pronouncing the word twice, saying: al-*hamdu* - al-*hamdu*; exceeding the terms of *Salaah*, and you would also find them in intensified pronunciation of the letter "**d**" in the word: 'al-magh<u>d</u>oub'". He said: "I have seen people trying to pronounce the letter '**d**' with intensity, and they ended up spitting. Iblis occupies such people with concentrating on the correctness of

## The Whispering of the Shaytan

pronunciation rather than understanding the recitation. It is all the effects of *waswasah* from Iblis."

Muhammad bin Qutaybah said regarding the problem of Qur'anic recitation: "People used to recite the Qur'an in their own language (Arabic), then other people from non-Arab lands, who did not master the language of the Qur'an, came. So, they rushed past many letters and hence distorted the rules of recitation. There was a man among them who was known for his righteousness; however I have never heard a more unsteady recitation. He confused the letters; by pronouncing the first one well, and the next one badly. He introduced other ways of pronouncing some letters, which differed from the recitation of Arabic speakers of the Arabian Peninsula. He imposed his hard and confused recitation upon his students, while Allah ﷻ and His Prophet ﷺ made everything easy for the Ummah.

The amazing thing is that he even imposed his recitation upon people when he led them in *Salaah*; forcing them to pray behind him.

When Ibn 'Uyaynah saw anyone praying using the recitation taught by that man, or was himself behind an Imam reciting the Qur'an with that confused recitation, he (Ibn 'Uyaynah) considered that the prayer should be redone, and many scholars agreed with his opinion, such as Bishr bin Al-Harith and Imam Ahmad bin Hanbal.

# The Whispering of the Shaytan

This was not the recitation of the Prophet ﷺ, nor the Companions and the followers after them, or the scholars of recitation. Rather, it was easy and gentle.

Al-Khallal said in *"Al-Jami'"*: "Abu Abdullah said: 'I do not like the recitation of that man (i.e. the same man mentioned by Ibn Qutaybah).'

It was reported that Ibn Al-Mubarak forbade Ar-Rabi' bin Anas to recite the Qur'an in that manner.

Al-Fadl bin Zayad said: "A man said to Abu Abdillah: 'What is to be avoided from his recitation?' He replied: 'Contraction (or assimilation) of letters, and fragmentation of words which was not known in any of the Arabic dialects."

Al-Hasan bin Muhammad bin Al-Harith asked him: "Do you hate that a man should learn such a recitation?" He replied: "I dislike it very much; it is an innovated recitation." He hated it so much that it made him furious.

It was narrated that Ibn Sunayd was asked about that recitation and he replied: "I hate it so much." It was said to him: "What is it you dislike about it?" he replied: "It is an innovated recitation, which no one has made before this."

Abdurrahman bin Mahdi said: "If I happened to perform *Salaah* behind an Imam with that recitation, I would certainly repeat it, once more."

# The Whispering of the Shaytan

Ahmad bin Hanbal stated that he would also have repeated *Salaah* behind an Imam with such a recitation. Yet another narration has stated that he would not repeat such a *Salaah*.

The important point here is that scholars disliked such recitations with intensified and innovated pronunciation of the letters of the Qur'an.

Whoever reflects on the guidance of the Prophet ﷺ would clearly see that all aspects of *waswasah* in pronouncing the letters of the Qur'an are not from his Sunnah.

## Reply to the Excuses of People Under the Influence of *Waswasah*

Their say: What we do is but a precaution not *waswasah*. We say: "Call it whatever you like. We simply ask you: 'Is it in accordance to the Sunnah of the Prophet ﷺ or his Companions? Or is it the opposite?'"

"If you claim that it is in accordance with the Sunnah, then it is a lie, and you should give up such a claim, and affirm that it is contradicting the Sunnah; therefore, you should not call it a precaution." This is similar to someone who commits an illegal act and calls it another

# The Whispering of the Shaytan

name; just as alcoholic drinks are given by different names, and usury is called trading.

It should be known that a precaution which benefits a person and grants him rewards from Allah ﷻ is a safety measure to act in conformity with the Sunnah of the Prophet ﷺ and an abstention from anything that opposes it.

Likewise, some people, in times of disputes, hastily announce divorce, which has been contested by scholars, regarding its legal opinion; such as an enforced divorce, divorce by a drunkard, divorce by *niyyah* (divorce by intention only), the postponed divorce (divorce with a pre-set date; planned), divorce with an oath (making an oath of divorce), and many other types of divorce which are largely disputed by scholars. If the *mufti* (judge) accepts the divorce just out of convention, without any proof, and says: this is a precaution against any illegal sexual intercourse, then he has indeed ignored the real meaning of precaution in this matter; because he forbade it for one and legalised it for another. Therefore, one may ask: "Where is the precaution in such a judgment?" Instead, if he does not rule the divorce, until there is majority ruling from the scholars of the Ummah about it (with a proof from the Book of Allah ﷻ and the Sunnah of the Prophet ﷺ), then we could say that he had acted with precautionary measures. This was the opinion of Imam Ahmad regarding the divorce announced by a drunkard.

# The Whispering of the Shaytan

Shaikh Ibn Taymiyah said: "Precaution is good, as long as it does not lead the *mufti* to contradict the Sunnah. If it does, then the "precautionary measure", in this case, is to leave aside that "precaution"."

This is the answer to their argumentation and excuses, with the Ahadith of the Prophet ﷺ who said: "Whoever saves himself from these suspicious things, saves his religion and his honour" and "Leave what causes you doubt, and turn what does not cause you doubt" and "A sin is that which weaves in the heart of someone." These Ahadith are great proof for invalidating *waswasah*.

It is in suspicious things that truth is compared with falsehood, the lawful with the unlawful, in a way that is not subjected to any proof for both sides. So the Prophet ﷺ has guided us to avoid what is suspicious and chose only the clear and obvious.

The objective of *Al-Waswas* (Satan) is to confuse the Muslim, whether his action is in line with the Sunnah or is it a *bid'ah* (an innovation)?

The clear and obvious way is to follow the way of the Prophet ﷺ and the guidelines he ﷺ set for his Ummah, in words and actions.

Whoever adopts the suspicious way, in his life has indeed disregarded the Sunnah and adopted *bid'ah*; he has abstained from pleasing Allah ﷻ and accepted what displeases Him ﷻ. he has distanced himself/herself from

# The Whispering of the Shaytan

Allah ﷻ, because the only way to get closer to Him ﷻ is by acing on His Co+mmands, not by one's own desires.

As for the date which the Messenger of Allah ﷺ abstained from eating, saying: "I fear that it might be a *sadaqah*" – as it was unlawful for the Prophet ﷺ and his household to eat from *sadaqah* – it was a prevention against suspicious things, where the lawful is confused with the unlawful. For, he ﷺ found the date in his house, and people used to bring dates to his place, so he ﷺ gave it away to poor people who deserved it. But, on the other hand, his family used to bring their own dates to the house, and so, he ﷺ did not know to which category of dates that particular one belonged. Therefore, he ﷺ abstained from eating it. This Hadith is a cause to cautiousness and prevention of suspicious things, but is not related to people of *waswasah* at all. Their argument is simply invalid.

As for your argument of Imam Malik's ruling, regarding one who announced divorce and did not remember whether it was the first or third, that it should be considered as the third out of precaution, we say: "Yes, this was the opinion of Malik. But should it become proof to be considered against the opinion of Shafi'i, Abu Haneefah, Imam Ahmad, or against all those who disagree with him in this issue? Does everyone have to give up their opinion and submit to his?"

This opinion is not related to *waswasah*, however its argument is: "Divorce necessitates the prohibition of the

# The Whispering of the Shaytan

wife (the wife does not become lawful to the husband), but *rij'ah* (remarriage with one's divorced wife, as long as the divorce was not the third) cancels the prohibition; as Imam Malik said: 'The reason of prohibition has been established, which is divorce.' But he had doubt regarding the remarriage, because, if it was not the final one (i.e. not the third divorce) then it could be cancelled by the possibility of remarriage. But if it happens to be the third and final one, then there is no possibility for remarrying one's divorced wife, and the prohibition is established in this case."

The majority of scholars have said: "Marriage is certain, so its cancellation is doubtful, because the *rij'ah* (return to one's wife) is possible; a fact which does not negate remarriage. Therefore, remarriage stands until there is confirmation of its negation."

If you say: "Prohibition of remarriage is certain, so its lawfulness is doubtful." We say: "*Rij'ah* is not unlawful to you, and so you legalise that sexual intercourse should become *rij'ah*, if one makes the intention for it to be so."
If you say: "Rather, it is unlawful, and *rij'ah* only took place with the intention at the time of the sexual intercourse." We say: "It is a poor argument which does not even support your opinion."

# The Whispering of the Shaytan

## Making an oath upon something for divorce

Whoever makes an oath for divorce, upon something (that there are two seeds in the nut, etc) which the swearing person is not certain about, and the result is different from what he thinks; such a person's oath is not broken according to many scholars.

Likewise, if the issue is not clear and remains unknown, then the marriage stands with certainty, and should not be negated by one's doubtfulness.

Imam Malik had a ruling which was contested by other scholars. It claimed that divorce could be established when an oath was doubtful, the way it is established when there is doubtfulness in the nature of divorce (whether it was first or second or final), as discussed earlier, and also the doubtfulness regarding a divorced wife, if her husband should announce that he had divorced one of his wives, yet forgotten whether it was the first or second or third announcement; in such case, divorce should take place. Exactly, when a man makes an oath about the identity of such and such a wife, while he has doubt in his mind. His oath is considered broken because of his state of doubtfulness, at the time of the oath.

# The Whispering of the Shaytan

The oath becomes broken when the result is different from what the oath was originally intended. If it is regarding a request, it becomes broken when a person does what he had sworn to give up, when making the oath. If it was based upon a piece of news, the oath is broken when the news is proven to be a lie.

Malik added another condition that may break an oath, (doubtfulness at the time of making the oath), whether it results in truth or not.

So, the decision is decided with the *hanath* (breaking one's oath), because of the existence of doubtfulness in it, as when someone makes an oath, then has doubt as to whether he had broken his oath or not. Maliki scholars would order him to be separated from his wife.

Is the decision an obligation or a recommendation?
There are two opinions; one of Ibn Al-Qasim, and the other of Malik:

Malik considered this as a continuation of the marriage.

Ibn Al-Qasim said: "As the state of marriage had become doubtful, so the husband should be separated from the wife."

However, the majority of scholars have said that he should not divorce her, nor is it recommended for him either; for the rule in *Shari'ah* says: doubtfulness is not a strong enough basis to remove the original known element; what is certain can only be removed by another element that is either stronger in certainty, or equal to it.

## The Ruling Regarding the Doubtful Divorce

As for a person who divorced one of his wives and forgot, or divorced one but did not mention her name; the scholars have differed in opinion over the ruling of this issue:

Abu Haneefah, Shafi'i, Thawri and Hammad said: "He chooses anyone he likes, and applies the divorce of the doubtful upon her. As for the state of the one he divorced and forgot, he should not come near any of his wives, but should spend on them all, until the matter is clarified. If he dies before he could find out which of his wives he had divorced and forgotten about, Abu Haneefah said that all his wives should then divide the legacy of that one wife with the others.

Shafi'i said: "The legacy should be suspended until they have made with one another." The Maliki school says: "If a husband divorces a non-nominated wife, saying: 'You are divorced,' but did not know which one; then his declaration applies on all of them. If he divorced one nominated wife, then later forgot which one it was, he should abstain from them all, until he remembers. If he

# The Whispering of the Shaytan

takes long, he should be given a deadline to remember; otherwise he should divorce them all. If he announces to his wives: one of you is divorced, but did not nominate her with intention, all of them should be divorced from him.

Imam Ahmad said: 'He chooses by lot among them in both cases'. This was stated by a group of his companions, and his narration was on the authority of Ali ؓ and Ibn 'Abbas ؓ. The clear opinion of this school is that there is no difference between the non-nominated divorced wife and the forgotten one.

Ibn Qudaamah said: "He chooses the non-nominated wife by lot. As for the forgotten one, he should abstain from all of his wives until the divorced one is known, and continues to spend on all of them. If he dies, lot-casting would decide between them for the outcome of the legacy."

Isma'il bin Ahmad reported, on the authority of Ahmad, that lot-casting should not be used regarding a forgotten wife, but it may be used to decide the outcome of the legacy. Isma'il said: "I asked Ahmad about a man who divorced one of his wives, but did not know which one he has divorced." He replied: "I would hate to make a divorce by lot-casting." I said: "What about if the man dies?" He replied: "I say decide by lot-casting, because it is applied to decide who receives the share of property."

# The Whispering of the Shaytan

## Doubts regarding purity

The legal opinion of Al-Hasan, Ibrahim An-Nakha'i, and Imam Malik (in one of his narrations), regarding a person who has doubt whether his ablution was invalidated or not, was that he should perform ablution again as a precautionary measure, and should not enter in *Salaah* in a state of doubtful purity. This issue is widely contested by the scholars.

The Majority of scholars, among them Shafi'i, Ahmad, Abu Haneefah and their companions, and Imam Malik in his other narration, have said that he should not perform ablution again, but can pray with the ablution he was certain he made yet had doubt about its validity.

They supported their opinion with a narration of Abu Hurayrah ؓ who said: "The Messenger of Allah ﷺ said: 'If any one of you has pain in his abdomen, but is doubtful whether or not anything has issued from him, he should not leave the mosque unless he hears a sound or perceives a smell." This applies to the one performing *Salaah* or otherwise.

Those of the first opinion say: One's state of *Salaah* is confirmed by one's lack of certainty, while one has doubt regarding the validity of one's *wudu'*. Therefore, as long as one is uncertain about its validity, one should not enter *Salaah* with doubt.

# The Whispering of the Shaytan

Others would say that it is a *Salaah* based on a known state of purity, the validity of which is doubtful. So, one should not pay attention to doubt, while there is still certainty. Likewise, if one has doubt whether one's clothes or body have been affected by an impurity, one should not wash them, as one would otherwise enter in *Salaah* with doubt.

They distinguished between them by using two interpretations:

First: that avoiding impurity is not a condition, therefore its *niyyah* (intention) is not obligatory. Rather, it is a preventive measure, that never existed from the beginning. Contrary to this *wudu'* is a principle element; so how can one even have doubt in its certainty.

Second: Before performing *wudu'*, he was in state of ritual impurity (due to using the toilet, etc.), which was his original state. So, if he has doubt about the validity of his *wudu'*, then one returns to the original state; therefore, but originality is not due to filth or any other type of impurity.

Others have said: The principle of impurity is removed by the certainty of purity, which becomes the original state or principle; so if we have doubt about purity, we return to it for our decision. How could this be compared to *waswasah*, which is shunned in the *Deen*, both in terms of reason and convention?

# The Whispering of the Shaytan

## What to do when not knowing the place of an impurity on one's clothing

As for the argument that if someone does not recognise the place of impurity on his clothing, he should wash all of it; it is not a case of *waswasah*. Rather it is a matter of fulfilling the necessary obligation. In this case, he should wash the part of his clothes which is impure; but since he does not know the spot, he should wash all the clothing to perform the obligation.

## Confusion in defining whether clothes are pure or impure

This is a disputed matter among the scholars.

Imam Malik, in one of his narrations, and Imam Ahmad said that, in this situation, one should pray in different clothes, in order to be sure of its purity. But the majority of scholars, and among them Abu Haneefah, Shafi'i, and Malik, in his other narration, said that one should examine the clothes and pray one *Salaah*, in one of the two clothes; this examination is similar to one's enquiry about the *Qiblah*.

Al-Muzni and Abu Thawr said that one should rather pray naked than pray in one of those clothes, because one

# The Whispering of the Shaytan

is forbidden to pray in impure clothes; therefore if one is unable to cover oneself with pure clothes, the obligation of covering is dropped. But this is the weakest of all opinions.

The opinion that is clear and more in favour is the one about examining one's clothes, whether the clean clothes were many or few; and this was the choice of Shaikh Ibn Taymiyyah. As for Ibn 'Uqayl, he said that if there were many clothes, one should follow the certainty of one's mind, but if there were only a few clothes, one should examine them al.

Sheikh Ibn Taymiyyah said: "Avoiding impurity is a matter of necessity; so if one has examined one's clothes, and thought of one of them as being pure, one should pray in them. His *Salaah* is not to be judged invalid because of doubtfulness."

The opinion of Abu Thawr (praying naked if uncertain about the purity of one's clothes) is completely invalid; for even if someone is certain about the impurity of his clothes, his *Salaah* in them is more appreciated to Allah ﷻ than praying naked, revealing the private parts before people.

In any case, this is not part of the reprehensible type of *waswasah*.

# The Whispering of the Shaytan

## Having doubt about the purity of containers used for ablution

Doubtf about the purity of vessels and containers is not an issue of *waswasah*, and scholars have differed greatly in their opinions about it.

Imam Ahmad said: "One should then perform *tayammum*, and not use the water in suspicious containers." In another narration, he said: "One should spill that water and perform *tayammum*, in order to be certain of not having any pure water to use."

Abu Haneefah said: "When the number of pure vessels exceeds that of impure ones, one should examine which one to use, but if they equal or are less in number than the impure ones, one does not have to examine them. This was also the opinion of some companions of Imam Ahmad, such as Abu Bakr, Ibn shaqilla and An-Najjad, the devout scholar who reported many narrations from Imam Ahmad.

Ash-Shafi'i and some Maliki scholars have said that one should examine the vessels in any situation.

A group of scholars, among them our sheikh, said that one should perform ablution using any of the containers, on the basis of the fact that water only becomes impure when it changes in taste or colour.

# The Whispering of the Shaytan

## Confusion of the direction of the *Qiblah*

The scholars have said that if one is confused about the direction of the *Qiblah*, one should follow one's own judgment, in the place where one happens to be, and then perform *Salaah*.

One scholar declared an unusual opinion when he said that in such a situation, one should pray four *Salaahs* in four directions. This is against the Sunnah; however the possessor of this opinion based his judgment on that of the confusion about the purity of one's clothes, but it remains unusual and should be disregarded.

## The Confusion of forgetting to pray one *Salaah* but not knowing which particular one

The scholars have differed in their opinion, regarding this issue.

First opinion: Ahmad, Malik, Ash-Shafi'i, Abu Haneefah and Ishaq, have said one should pray all five *Salaahs*, because one has no other way of being certain one has performed the right *Salaah*.

# The Whispering of the Shaytan

The second opinion: one should perform a *Salaah* of four *Raka'at*, intending to compensate for the forgotten one, but should sit to do the *tahiyyah* in all the *Raka'at*, and this was the opinion of Al-Awza'i, Zufar bin Al-Hudhayl, and Muammad bin Muqatil from the Hanafi school.

The third opinion: to compensate for a forgotten but unknown *Salaah*, one should pray one *Salaah Fajr*, one *Maghrib* and one of four Raka'at, with the intention to cover the one he has forgotten, and this was the opinion of Sufiyan Ath-Thawri and Muhammad bin Al-Hasan.

As for Abdullah bin Ahmad, he said: "I heard my father being questioned: 'What do you do about a person who was reminded that he had forgotten a *Salaah*, so he prayed two *raka'at*, did *tashahud*, made the intention for it to be that of the early morning prayer, but did not yet make *Salam*; then stood up, prayed one *raka'ah*, made *tashahud*, and intended for it to cover a *Maghrib* prayer; then stood up again, prayed a fourth *raka'ah*, made *tashahud* and intended for it to cover a *Dhuhr* (noon) or '*Asr* (afternoon) prayer and ended with *salam*?' My father replied: 'This would compensate for and cover his forgotten *Salaah*."

# The Whispering of the Shaytan

## Invalidating the proofs of people under the influence of waswasah

If anyone has doubt in his *Salaah*, he should base his decision upon the certainty of his mind.

As for forbidding the eating of game, if one had doubts as to whether it died of wounds or in water, or forbids its eating if one's dogs were mixed with someone else's dogs, the Prophet ﷺ commanded that in such cases the eating should be forbidden, because one had doubt in the reason of its lawfulness, while the animal was originally forbidden. Therefore, it should not be legalised with doubt (on the condition of its lawfulness), which is contrary to when the animal was originally lawful; as it does not become unlawful with doubt. It is similar to when someone buys some water, food or clothes, yet does not know its condition, (whether or not it is lawful to use any of them) and has doubt about its purity; if the original state of the element is lawfulness, then one should disregard doubt.

For example: if someone was given some meat, but did not know its origin; whether it was slaughtered according to Shari'ah or not, the meat in this case is lawful to consume, because of the difficulty of investigating its origin. 'Aishah asked the Prophet ﷺ: "O Messenger of Allah, some rural Arab people bring meat to us, but we do not know whether they mentioned the Name of Allah

# The Whispering of the Shaytan

before slaughtering the animal or not? He ﷺ replied: "Mention the name of Allah (yourselves) and eat."

In the second example about water, food and clothing, the original state of these things was pure, so one need only doubt about the existence of some form of impurity, therefore, one should disregard one's doubt.

## *Waswasah* of Ibn 'Umar ؓ in ablution

As for what some people (the argument of those under the influence of *waswasah*) mentioned about Ibn 'Umar ؓ and Abu Hurayrah ؓ, it was something which they were uniquely singled out with, and none of the Companions ؓ agreed with Ibn 'Umar ؓ about it. Ibn 'Umar, himself, used to say: "I am under the influence of *waswasah*, so do not take me as an example."

The apparent interpretation of the school of Shafi'i and that of Ahmad is that it is not recommended to wash inside one's eyes in ablution, even if there is no harm involved; because it was never reported about the Prophet ﷺ that he did this, nor commanded anyone to do so. The Prophet's ablution was reported by many of his Companions, such as 'Uthman, Ali 'Abdullah bin Zayd, Rubayyi' bint Mu'awidh ؓ and others; none of them said that he ﷺ used to wash inside his eyes.

# The Whispering of the Shaytan

As for the obligation to wash the eyes in *Janabah*[1], there are two narrations from Imam Ahmad, and the correct one is that it is not an obligation, which is also the opinion of the majority of scholars. Therefore, it is not an obligation to wash inside the eyes from impurity, because they are more likely to be harmed than cleaned.

The Shafi'i and Hanafi Schools claim that it is necessary to wash them; since they are rarely affected by impurity, so it is not difficult to clean them.

Some scholars of the companions of Imam Ahmad exaggerated even more, when they suggested that the eyes should be cleaned in ablution. This opinion should be ignored, as the correct one is that it is not an obligation to wash one's eyes, either for ablution, from *Janabah*, or any impurity.

As for Abu Hurayrah ﷺ, it was his own interpretation, and many scholars have disagreed with him. This issue was called the extension of *al-ghurrah*[2], despite the fact that *al-ghurrah* is particularly related to the face.

There are two narrations from Ahmad regarding this issue:

---

[1] Major ritual impurity.
[2] Literally, it means the white spot on a horse's face; while in this context, it means the light of the believer and the ornamentation of those parts of the body, where ablution were made, on the Day of Resurrection.

# The Whispering of the Shaytan

First: it is recommended to extend the method of ablution, and this was the same opinion of Abu Haneefah and Shafi'i, and it was also the choice of Abu Al-Barakaat Ibn Taymiyyah and others.

Second: It is not recommended, and this was the opinion of the Maliki school, and the choice of our Shaikh, Abu Al-'Abbas.

Those who have recommended the extension in ablution have supported their opinion with the Hadith, reported by Abu Hurayrah ﷺ who said: "The Messenger of Allah said: 'In a believer, adornment would reach the places where ablution reaches.'"[1]

Those who had denied the recommendation have said: "The Prophet ﷺ said: 'Allah ﷻ had set boundaries; so do not exceed them.'"[2] Allah ﷻ set the washing of the arms and feet, in ablution, to the elbow and ankle; therefore, one should not wash beyond them in one's ablution. Furthermore, it was never reported that the Prophet ﷺ washed beyond those limits in his ablution; so the origin of this exaggeration is *waswasah*, which entices one to do it as an act of worship to get closer to Allah ﷻ. But worshipping Allah ﷻ properly is based on following the Sunnah of His Prophet ﷺ, not exaggerating in any act. Neither the Prophet ﷺ nor his Companions had ever

---
[1] Recorded by Muslim.
[2] Recorded by Imam Ahmad, Daraqutni, on the authority of Abu Tha'labah Al-Khashni. An-Nawawi said: "The Hadith is classified as *Hasan*."

## The Whispering of the Shaytan

exaggerated in their *wudu'*, and he ﷺ once said: "O people, beware of the excessiveness in *Deen*."[1]

The Hadith of Abu Hurayrah ؓ above was reported by Nu'aym Al-Mujmir, who said: "I do not know whether the saying: 'Whoever is able to extend washing his organ in *wudu'* may do so' was that of the Prophet ﷺ or of Abu Hurayrah ؓ."[2]

As for the Hadith of the ornament, the ornament of beautification is the one applied to its place; so if it exceeds its place, it is no longer an ornament.

## A reply to those who say that *waswasah* is better than taking things for granted

You have claimed that being under the influence of *waswasah* (and doing things beyond the standard or boundaries set by the Prophet ﷺ) was better than being negligent, and not taking matters seriously. But such actions represent negligence and exaggeration, excessiveness and laxity, extravagance and miserliness, and Allah ﷻ has forbidden both facts in many Verses in the Qur'an, when He ﷻ said:

---

[1] Recorded by Ahmad, An-Nassa'i, Ibn Maajah and Al-Haakim on the authority of Ibn 'Abbas ؓ
[2] This was reported by Imam Ahmad in his "Musnad".

## The Whispering of the Shaytan

⟨And do not let your hands be tied to your neck, nor stretch it forth to its utmost reach⟩[1]

⟨Do not spend wastefully in the manner of a spendthrift⟩[2]

⟨And those who, when they spend, are neither extravagant nor niggardly, but hold a medium way between those extremes⟩[3]

⟨And eat and drink but do not waste in extravagance⟩[4]

The *Deen* of Allah ﷻ is between the excessiveness and the negligence, and the best people are the middle type, who avoid the negligence of careless people, and refrain from joining excessive people and transgressors. For Allah ﷻ made the Muslim Ummah a balanced community, which is a just choice, because of its middle position, between a reprehensible state (of excess and negligence) and justice, which is an intermediate state between them.

---

[1] Surat Al-Isra', verse 29.
[2] Surat Al-Isra', verse 26.
[3] Surat Al-Furqan, verse 67.
[4] Surat Al-A'raf, verse 31.

# The Whispering of the Shaytan

This was about the stratagems of Satan, and his influence in our Ummah, so that sincere Muslims may know the merit of having *'ilm* (knowledge) and *Iman* (faith), so as to understand all the Blessing of Allah ﷻ upon them.

Allah ﷻ guides, through His Blessings, whoever He ﷻ wishes, from those seeking the truth in this Ummah, as success and right guidance are from Allah ﷻ.

This is the conclusion of this book; so whatever is right (in it) is from Allah ﷻ, Alone, and whatever is wrong (in it) is from the author and Satan.

I ask Allah ﷻ to make this a sincere effort, seeking His Pleasure, and I ask Him ﷻ to grant us refuge in Him from the evils within ourselves, and that in our deeds. I ask Him ﷻ to grant us success in achieving whatever pleases Him; He ﷻ is close and responsive (to the prayers of His faithful Servants).

All Praise to Allah, the Lord of the Universe; and may His *Salaah* be upon Prophet Muhammad ﷺ, his family and all his Companions ﵀.

www.ingramcontent.com/pod-product-compliance
Lightning Source LLC
Chambersburg PA
CBHW071023080526
44587CB00015B/2474